Djurdja Jovanovic Padejski

FRANCIS FUKUYAMA is Olivier Nomellini Senior
Fellow at Stanford University's Freeman Spogli
Institute for International Studies and Mosbacher
Director of its Center on Democracy, Development, and the Rule of Law. He has previously
taught at the Paul H. Nitze School of Advanced
International Studies at Johns Hopkins University and at the George Mason University School
of Public Policy. Fukuyama was a researcher at
the RAND Corporation and served as the deputy
director for the State Department's policy of
planning staff. He is the author of *Political Order
and Political Decay*, *The Origins of Political Order*, *The End of History and the Last Man*, *Trust*,
and *America at the Crossroads: Democracy, Power,
and the Neoconservative Legacy*. He lives with his
wife in California.

IDENTITY

IDENTITY

IDENTITY

THE

DEMAND FOR DIGNITY

AND THE

POLITICS OF RESENTMENT

FRANCIS FUKUYAMA

PICADOR | FARRAR, STRAUS AND GIROUX | NEW YORK

picadorusa.com • instagram.com/picador
twitter.com/picadorusa • facebook.com/picadorusa

Picador® is a U.S. registered trademark and is used by Macmillan Publishing Group, LLC, under license from Pan Books Limited.

For book club information, please visit facebook.com/picadorbookclub or email marketing@picadorusa.com.

Designed by Abby Kagan

The Library of Congress has cataloged
the Farrar, Straus and Giroux edition as follows:

Names: Fukuyama, Francis, author.
Title: Identity : the demand for dignity and the politics of resentment / Francis Fukuyama.
Description: First edition. | New York : Farrar, Straus and Giroux, 2018. | Includes bibliographical references and index.
Identifiers: LCCN 2018004954 | ISBN 9780374129293 (hardcover) | ISBN 9780374717483 (ebook)
Subjects: LCSH: Political participation—Social aspects. | Identity politics. | Group identity—Political aspects. | Dignity. | Resentment. | Polarization (Social sciences)—Political aspects. | World politics—21st century.
Classification: LCC JF799 .F85 2018 | DDC 320.01/9—dc23
LC record available at https://lccn.loc.gov/2018004954

Picador Paperback ISBN 978-1-250-23464-3

Our books may be purchased in bulk for promotional, educational, or business use. Please contact your local bookseller or the Macmillan Corporate and Premium Sales Department at 1-800-221-7945, extension 5442, or by email at MacmillanSpecialMarkets@macmillan.com.

First published by Farrar, Straus and Giroux

First Picador Edition: September 2019

D   10   9   8   7   6

For Julia, David, and John

CONTENTS

PREFACE

This book would not have been written had Donald J. Trump not been elected president in November 2016. Like many Americans, I was surprised by this outcome and troubled by its implications for the United States and the world. It was the second major electoral surprise of that year, the first being Britain's vote to leave the European Union the previous June.

I had spent much of the last couple decades thinking about the development of modern political institutions: how the state, rule of law, and democratic accountability first came into being, how they evolved and interacted, and, finally, how they could decay. Well before Trump's election, I had written that American institutions were decaying as the state was progressively captured by powerful interest groups and locked into a rigid structure that was unable to reform itself.

Trump himself was both the product of and a contributor to that decay. The promise of his candidacy was that, as an outsider, he would use his popular mandate to shake up the system and make it functional again. Americans were tired of partisan gridlock and yearning for a strong leader who could unite the country again, breaking through what I labeled vetocracy—the ability of interest groups to block collective action. This kind of populist upsurge was what put Franklin D. Roosevelt into the White House in 1932 and reshaped American politics for the next two generations.

The problem with Trump was twofold, having to do with both policy and character. His economic nationalism was likely to make things worse rather than better for the very constituencies that supported him, while his evident preference for authoritarian strongmen over democratic allies promised to destabilize the entire international order. With regard to character, it was hard to imagine an individual less suited to be president of the United States. The virtues that one associates with great leadership—basic honesty, reliability, sound judgment, devotion to public interest, and an underlying moral compass—were totally missing. Trump's primary focus throughout his career had been on self-promotion, and he was perfectly happy to get around people or rules that stood in his way by any means available.

Trump represented a broader trend in international politics, toward what has been labeled populist nationalism.[1] Populist leaders seek to use the legitimacy conferred by democratic elections to consolidate power. They claim direct charismatic connection to "the people," who are often defined in narrow ethnic terms that exclude big parts of the population. They don't like institutions and seek to undermine the checks and balances that limit a leader's personal power in a modern liberal democracy: courts, the legislature, an independent media, and a nonpartisan bureaucracy. Other contemporary leaders who could be put in this category are Vladimir Putin of Russia, Recep Tayyip Erdoğan of Turkey, Viktor Orbán of Hungary, Jaroslaw Kaczynski of Poland, and Rodrigo Duterte of the Philippines.

The global surge toward democracy that began in the mid-1970s has gone into what my colleague Larry Diamond calls a global recession.[2] In 1970, there were only about 35 electoral democracies, a number that steadily increased over the next three decades until it reached nearly 120 by the early 2000s. The greatest acceleration came from 1989 to 1991, when the collapse of Communism in Eastern Europe and the former Soviet Union led to a democratic wave throughout that region. Since the mid-2000s, however, the trend has reversed itself, and total numbers have declined. Authoritarian countries, led by China, have meanwhile grown more confident and self-assertive.

It is not surprising that new would-be democracies such as Tunisia, Ukraine, and Myanmar should be struggling to build workable institutions, or that liberal democracy failed to take root in Afghanistan or Iraq after the U.S. interventions in those countries. It is disappointing, though not wholly surprising, that Russia has reverted to authoritarian traditions. What was far more unexpected was that threats to democracy should arise from within established democracies themselves. Hungary had been one of the first countries in Eastern Europe to overthrow its Communist regime. When it entered both NATO and the European Union, it appeared to have rejoined Europe as what political scientists characterized as a "consolidated" liberal democracy. Yet under Orbán and his Fidesz party, it has been leading the way toward what Orbán has labeled "illiberal democracy." But a far bigger surprise yet were the votes in Britain and the United States for Brexit and Trump, respectively.

These were the two leading democracies that had been the architects of the modern liberal international order, countries that led the "neoliberal" revolution under Ronald Reagan and Margaret Thatcher during the 1980s. Yet they themselves appeared to be turning away toward a more narrow nationalism.

This brings me to the origins of the present volume. Ever since I published my essay "The End of History?" in mid-1989, and the book *The End of History and the Last Man* in 1992,[3] I have regularly been asked whether event X didn't invalidate my thesis. X could be a coup in Peru, war in the Balkans, the September 11 attacks, the global financial crisis, or, most recently, Donald Trump's election and the wave of populist nationalism described above.

Most of these criticisms were based on a simple misunderstanding of the thesis. I was using the word *history* in the Hegelian-Marxist sense—that is, the long-term evolutionary story of human institutions that could alternatively be labeled *development* or *modernization*. The word *end* was meant not in the sense of "termination," but "target" or "objective." Karl Marx had suggested that the end of history would be a communist utopia, and I was simply suggesting that Hegel's version, where development resulted in a liberal state linked to a market economy, was the more plausible outcome.[4]

This didn't mean that my views hadn't changed over the years. The fullest rethinking I have been able to provide is contained in my two volumes *The Origins of Political Order* and *Political Order and Political Decay*, which might collectively be understood as an effort to rewrite *The End of History and the Last Man* based on what I understand of world politics now.[5] The two most important changes in my thinking concern, first, the difficulty of developing a modern, impersonal state—the problem I referred to as "getting to Denmark"—and second, the possibility of a modern liberal democracy decaying or going backward.

However, my critics missed another point. They did not note that the original essay had a question mark at the end of the title, and they did not read the later chapters of *The End of History and the Last Man* that focused on the problem of Nietzsche's Last Man.

In both places I noted that neither nationalism nor religion were about to disappear as forces in world politics. They were not about to disappear because, I argued back then, contemporary liberal democracies had not fully solved the problem of *thymos*. Thymos is the part of the soul that craves recognition of dignity; *isothymia* is the demand to be respected on an equal basis with other people; while *megalothymia* is the desire to be recognized as superior. Modern liberal democracies promise and largely deliver a minimal degree of equal respect, embodied in individual rights, the rule of law, and the franchise. What this does not guarantee is that people in a democracy will be equally respected in practice, particularly members of groups with a history of marginalization. Entire countries can feel disrespected, which has powered aggressive nationalism, as can religious believers who feel their faith is denigrated. Isothymia will therefore continue to drive demands for equal recognition, which are unlikely to ever be completely fulfilled.

The other big problem is megalothymia. Liberal democracies have been pretty good at providing peace and prosperity (though somewhat less so in recent years). These wealthy, secure societies are the domain of Nietzsche's Last Man, "men without chests" who spend their lives in the endless pursuit of consumer satisfaction, but who have nothing at their core, no higher goals or ideals for which they are willing to strive and sacrifice. Such a life will not satisfy everyone. Megalothymia thrives on exceptionality: taking big risks, engaging in monumental struggles, seeking large effects, because all of these lead to recognition of oneself as superior to others. In some cases, it can lead to a heroic leader like a Lincoln or a Churchill or a Nelson Mandela. But in other cases, it can lead to tyrants like Caesar or Hitler or Mao who lead their societies into dictatorship and disaster.

Since megalothymia has historically existed in all societies, it cannot be overcome; it can only be channeled or moderated. The question I raised in the final chapter of *The End of History and the Last Man* was whether the modern system of liberal democracy tied to a market economy would provide sufficient outlets for megalothymia. This problem was fully recognized by the American founding fathers. In their effort to create a republican form of government in North America, they were aware of the history of the fall of the Roman Republic and worried about the problem of Caesarism. Their solution was the constitutional system of checks and balances that would distribute power and block its concentration in a single leader. Back in 1992, I suggested that a market economy also provided outlets for megalothymia. An entrepreneur could become fabulously wealthy while contributing at the same time to general prosperity. Or such individuals could compete in Ironman events or set records for the number of Himalayan peaks climbed or build the world's most valuable internet company.

I actually mentioned Donald Trump in *The End of History* as an example of a fantastically ambitious individual whose desire for recognition had been safely channeled into a business (and later an entertainment) career. Little did I suspect back then that, twenty-five years on, he would not be satisfied with business success and celebrity, but would go into politics and get elected president. But it is not at all inconsistent with the general argument I was making about potential future threats to liberal democracy, and the central problem of thymos in a liberal society.[6] Such figures had existed in the past with names such as Caesar or Hitler or Perón, who had led their societies down disastrous paths to war or economic decline. To propel themselves forward, such figures latched onto the resentments of ordinary people who felt that their nation or religion or way of life was being disrespected. Megalothymia and isothymia thus joined hands.

In the present volume I am returning to themes that I began to explore in 1992 and have been writing about ever since: thymos, recognition, dignity, identity, immigration, nationalism, religion, and culture. In particular, it incorporates the Lipset Memorial Lecture on immigration and identity that I gave in 2005, and the Latsis Foundation lecture I delivered in Geneva in 2011 on immigration and European identity.[7] In some places this volume more or less repeats passages from earlier writings. I apologize if any of this seems repetitious, but I'm pretty confident that few people have taken the time to follow this particular string and to see it as a coherent argument relating to developments in the present.

Demand for recognition of one's identity is a master concept that unifies much of what is going on in world politics today. It is not confined to the identity politics practiced on university campuses, or to the white nationalism it has provoked, but extends to broader phenomena such as the upsurge of old-fashioned nationalism and politicized Islam. Much of what passes for economic motivation is, I will argue, actually rooted in the demand for recognition and therefore cannot simply be satisfied by economic means. This has direct implications for how we should deal with populism in the present.

According to Hegel, human history was driven by a struggle

for recognition. He argued that the only rational solution to the desire for recognition was universal recognition, in which the dignity of every human being was recognized. Universal recognition has been challenged ever since by other partial forms of recognition based on nation, religion, sect, race, ethnicity, or gender, or by individuals wanting to be recognized as superior. The rise of identity politics in modern liberal democracies is one of the chief threats that they face, and unless we can work our way back to more universal understandings of human dignity, we will doom ourselves to continuing conflict.

I would like to thank a number of friends and colleagues for providing comments on this manuscript: Sheri Berman, Gerhard Casper, Patrick Chamorel, Mark Cordover, Katherine Cramer, Larry Diamond, Bob Faulkner, Jim Fearon, David Fukuyama, Sam Gill, Anna Gryzmala-Busse, Margaret Levi, Mark Lilla, Kate McNamara, Yascha Mounk, Marc Plattner, Lee Ross, Susan Shell, Steve Stedman, and Kathryn Stoner.

Special thanks are due to Eric Chinski, my editor at Farrar, Straus and Giroux, who has worked tirelessly with me on several books now. His sense of logic and language and his wide knowledge of substantive issues have been of enormous benefit to the current volume. I am also thankful for the support given me by Andrew Franklin at Profile Books for this and all previous volumes.

As always, I am grateful to my literary agents, Esther Newberg at International Creative Management and Sophie Baker at Curtis Brown, as well as to all the other people who support them. They have done amazing work in getting my books published in the United States and all over the world.

I would also like to thank my research assistants Ana Urgiles, Eric Gilliam, Russell Clarida, and Nicole Southard, who were invaluable in providing materials on which the book is based.

I'm grateful for the support of my family and especially my wife, Laura, who has been a careful reader and critic of all my books.

Palo Alto and Carmel-by-the-Sea, California

IDENTITY

1
THE POLITICS OF DIGNITY

Sometime in the middle of the second decade of the twenty-first century, world politics changed dramatically.

The period from the early 1970s through the mid-2000s witnessed what Samuel Huntington labeled the "third wave" of democratization as the number of countries that could be classified as electoral democracies increased from about 35 to more than 110. In this period, liberal democracy became the default form of government for much of the world, at least in aspiration if not in practice.[1]

In parallel to this shift in political institutions was a corresponding growth of economic interdependence among nations, or what we call globalization. The latter was underpinned by liberal economic institutions such as the General Agreement on Tariffs and Trade and its successor, the World Trade Organization. These were supplemented by regional trade agreements such as the European Union and the North American Free Trade Agreement. Throughout this period, the rate of growth in international trade and investment outpaced global GDP growth and was widely seen as the major driver of prosperity. Between 1970 and 2008, the world's output of goods and services quadrupled and growth extended to virtually all regions of the world, while the number of people living in extreme poverty in developing countries dropped from 42 percent of the total population in 1993 to 17 percent in 2011. The percentage of children dying before their fifth birthdays declined from 22 percent in 1960 to less than 5 percent by 2016.[2]

This liberal world order did not, however, benefit everyone. In many countries around the world, and particularly in developed democracies, inequality increased dramatically, such that many of the benefits of growth flowed primarily to an elite defined primarily by education.[3] Since growth was related to the increasing volume of goods, money, and people moving from one place to another, there was a huge amount of disruptive social change. In developing countries, villagers who previously had no access to electricity suddenly found themselves living in large cities, watching TV or connected to the internet via ubiquitous cell phones. Labor markets adjusted to new conditions by driving tens of millions of people across international borders in search of better opportunities for themselves and their families, or else seeking to escape intolerable conditions at home. Huge new middle classes arose in countries such as China and India, but the work they did replaced work that had been done by older middle classes in the developed world. Manufacturing moved steadily from Europe and the United States to East Asia and other low-labor-cost regions. At the same time, women were displacing men in an increasingly service-dominated new economy, and low-skilled workers were being replaced by smart machines.

Beginning in the mid-2000s, the momentum toward an

increasingly open and liberal world order began to falter, then went into reverse. This shift coincided with two financial crises, the first originating in the U.S. subprime market in 2008 that led to the subsequent Great Recession, and the second emerging over the threat to the euro and the European Union posed by Greece's insolvency. In both cases, elite policies produced huge recessions, high levels of unemployment, and falling incomes for millions of ordinary workers around the world. Since the United States and the EU were the leading exemplars, these crises damaged the reputation of liberal democracy as a whole.

The democracy scholar Larry Diamond has characterized the years after the crises as ones of a "democratic recession," in which the aggregate number of democracies fell from their peak in virtually all regions of the world.[4] A number of authoritarian countries, led by China and Russia, became much more self-confident and assertive: China began promoting its "China model" as a path to development and wealth that was distinctly undemocratic, while Russia attacked the liberal decadence of the European Union and the United States. A number of countries that had seemed to be successful liberal democracies during the 1990s slid backward toward more authoritarian government, including Hungary, Turkey, Thailand, and Poland. The Arab Spring of 2011 disrupted dictatorships throughout the Middle East, but then profoundly disappointed hopes for greater democracy in the region as Libya, Yemen, Iraq, and Syria descended into civil war. The terrorist upsurge that produced the September 11 attacks was not defeated by the U.S. invasions of Afghanistan and Iraq. Rather, it mutated into the Islamic State, which emerged as a beacon for profoundly illiberal and violent Islamists around the world. What was as remarkable as ISIS's resilience was that so many young Muslims left lives of comparative safety elsewhere in the Middle East and Europe to travel to Syria to fight on its behalf.

More surprising and perhaps even more significant were the two big electoral surprises of 2016, Britain's vote to leave the European Union and the election of Donald J. Trump as president of the United States. In both cases, voters were concerned with economic issues, particularly those in the working class who had been exposed to job loss and deindustrialization. But just as important was opposition to continued large-scale immigration, which was seen as taking jobs from native-born workers and eroding long-established cultural identities. Anti-immigrant and anti-EU parties gained strength in many other developed countries, most notably the National Front in France, the Party for Freedom in the Netherlands, the Alternative for Germany, and the Freedom Party in Austria. Across the Continent there were both fears of Islamist terrorism and controversies over bans on expressions of Muslim identity such as the burka, niqab, and burkini.

Twentieth-century politics had been organized along a left–right spectrum defined by economic issues, the left wanting more equality and the right demanding greater freedom. Progressive politics centered around workers, their trade unions, and social democratic parties that sought better social protections and economic redistribution. The right by contrast was primarily interested in reducing the size of government and promoting the private sector. In the second decade of the twenty-first century, that spectrum appears to be giving way in many regions to one defined by identity. The left has focused less on broad economic equality and more on promoting the interests of a wide variety of groups perceived as being marginalized— blacks, immigrants, women, Hispanics, the LGBT community, refugees, and the like. The right, meanwhile, is redefining itself as patriots who seek to protect traditional national identity, an identity that is often explicitly connected to race, ethnicity, or religion.

A long tradition dating back at least as far as Karl Marx sees political struggles as a reflection of economic conflicts, essentially as fights over shares of the pie. Indeed, this is part of the story of the 2010s, with globalization producing significant populations of people left behind by the overall growth that occurred around the world. Between 2000 and 2016, half of Americans saw no gains to their real incomes; the proportion of national output going to the top 1 percent went from 9 percent of GDP in 1974 to 24 percent in 2008.[5]

But as important as material self-interest is, human beings are motivated by other things as well, motives that better explain the disparate events of the present. This might be called the politics of resentment. In a wide variety of cases, a political leader has mobilized followers around the perception that the group's dignity had been affronted, disparaged, or otherwise disregarded. This resentment engenders demands for public recognition of the dignity of the group in question. A humiliated group seeking restitution of its dignity carries far more emotional weight than people simply pursuing their economic advantage.

Thus, Russian president Vladimir Putin has talked about the tragedy of the collapse of the former Soviet Union, and how Europe and the United States had taken advantage of Russia's weakness during the 1990s to drive NATO up to its borders. He despises the attitude of moral superiority of Western politicians and wants to see Russia treated not, as President Obama once said, as a weak regional player, but as a great power. Viktor Orbán, the Hungarian prime minister, stated in 2017 that his return to power in 2010 marked the point when "we Hungarians also decided that we wanted to regain our country, we wanted to regain our self-esteem, and we wanted to regain our future."[6] The Chinese government of Xi Jinping has talked at length about China's "one hundred years of humiliation," and how the United States, Japan, and other countries were trying to prevent its return to the great power status it had enjoyed through the past millennia of history. When the founder of al-Qaeda, Osama bin Laden, was fourteen, his mother found him fixated on Palestine, "tears streaming down his face as he watched TV from their home in Saudi Arabia."[7] His anger at the humiliation of Muslims was later echoed by his young coreligionists volunteering to fight in Syria on behalf of a faith they believed had been attacked and oppressed around the world. They hoped to re-create the glories of an earlier Islamic civilization in the Islamic State.

Resentment at indignities was a powerful force in democratic countries as well. The Black Lives Matter movement sprang from a series of well-publicized police killings of African-Americans in Ferguson (Missouri), Baltimore, New York, and other cities and sought to force the outside world to pay attention to the experience of the victims of seemingly casual police violence. On college campuses and in offices around the country, sexual assault and sexual harassment were seen as evidence of men not taking women seriously as equals. Sudden attention was paid to transgender people, who had previously not been recognized as a distinct target of discrimination. And many of those who voted for Donald Trump remembered a better time in the past when their place in their own societies was more secure and hoped through their actions to "make America great again." While distant in time and place, the feelings among Putin's supporters over the arrogance and contempt of Western elites were similar to those experienced by rural voters in the United States who felt that the urban bicoastal elites and their media allies were similarly ignoring them and their problems.

The practitioners of the politics of resentment recognize one another. The sympathy that Vladimir Putin and Donald Trump have for each other is not just personal, but rooted in their common nationalism. Viktor Orbán explained, "Certain theories describe the changes now taking place in the Western world and the emergence on the stage of a U.S. president as a struggle in the world political arena between the transnational elite—referred to as 'global'—and patriotic national elites," of which he was an early exemplar.[8]

In all cases a group, whether a great power such as Russia or China or voters in the United States or Britain, believes that it has an identity that is not being given adequate recognition—either by the outside world, in the case of a nation, or by other members of the same society. Those identities can be and are incredibly varied, based on nation, religion, ethnicity, sexual orientation, or gender. They are all manifestations of a common phenomenon, that of identity politics.

The terms *identity* and *identity politics* are of fairly recent provenance, the former having been popularized by the psychologist Erik Erikson during the 1950s, and the latter coming into view only in the cultural politics of the 1980s and '90s. Identity has a wide number of meanings today, in some cases referring simply to social categories or roles, in others to basic information about oneself (as in "my identity was stolen"). Used in this fashion, identities have always existed.[9]

In this book, I will be using *identity* in a specific sense that helps us understand why it is so important to contemporary politics. Identity grows, in the first place, out of a distinction between one's true inner self and an outer world of social rules and norms that does not adequately recognize that inner self's worth or dignity. Individuals throughout human history have found themselves at odds with their societies. But only in modern times has the view taken hold that the authentic inner self is intrinsically valuable, and the outer society systematically wrong and unfair in its valuation of the former. It is not the inner self that has to be made to conform to society's rules, but society itself that needs to change.

The inner self is the basis of human dignity, but the nature of that dignity is variable and has changed over time. In many early cultures, dignity is attributed only to a few people, often warriors who are willing to risk their lives in battle. In other societies, dignity is an attribute of all human beings, based on their intrinsic worth as people with agency. And in other cases, dignity is due to one's membership in a larger group of shared memory and experience.

Finally, the inner sense of dignity seeks recognition. It is not enough that I have a sense of my own worth if other people do not publicly acknowledge it or, worse yet, if they denigrate me or don't acknowledge my existence. Self-esteem arises out of esteem by others. Because human beings naturally crave recognition, the modern sense of identity evolves quickly into identity politics, in which individuals demand public recognition of their worth. Identity politics thus encompasses a large part of the political struggles of the contemporary world, from democratic revolutions to new social movements, from nationalism and Islamism to the politics on contemporary American university campuses. Indeed, the philosopher Hegel argued that the struggle for recognition was the ultimate driver of human history, a force that was key to understanding the emergence of the modern world.

While the economic inequalities arising from the last fifty

or so years of globalization are a major factor explaining contemporary politics, economic grievances become much more acute when they are attached to feelings of indignity and disrespect. Indeed, much of what we understand to be economic motivation actually reflects not a straightforward desire for wealth and resources, but the fact that money is perceived to be a marker of status and buys respect. Modern economic theory is built around the assumption that human beings are rational individuals who all want to maximize their "utility"—that is, their material well-being—and that politics is simply an extension of that maximizing behavior. However, if we are ever to properly interpret the behavior of real human beings in the contemporary world, we have to expand our understanding of human motivation beyond this simple economic model that so dominates much of our discourse. No one contests that human beings are capable of rational behavior, or that they are self-interested individuals who seek greater wealth and resources. But human psychology is much more complex than the rather simpleminded economic model suggests. Before we can understand contemporary identity politics, we need to step back and develop a deeper and richer understanding of human motivation and behavior. We need, in other words, a better theory of the human soul.

2

THE THIRD PART OF THE SOUL

Theories of politics have typically been built on top of theories of human behavior. Theories tease out regularities in human action from the mass of empirical information we receive about the world around us and hopefully draw causal connections between these actions and the surrounding environment. The ability to theorize is an important factor in the evolutionary success of the human species. Many practical people scorn theories and theorizing, but they act all the time upon unarticulated theories that they simply fail to acknowledge.

Modern economics is based on one such theory, which is that human beings are "rational utility maximizers": they are individuals who use their formidable cognitive abilities to benefit their self-interest. Embedded in this theory are several further assumptions. One is that the unit of account is an individual, as opposed to a family, a tribe, a nation, or some other type of social group. To the extent that people cooperate with one another, it is because they calculate that cooperation will serve their individual self-interest better than if they act on their own.

The second assumption concerns the nature of "utility," the individual preferences—for a car, for sexual gratification, for a pleasant vacation—that make up what economists call a person's "utility function." Many economists would argue that their science says nothing about the ultimate preferences or utilities that people choose; that's up to individuals. Economics speaks only to the ways in which preferences are rationally pursued. Thus a hedge fund manager seeking to earn another billion dollars and a soldier who falls on a grenade to save his buddies are both maximizing their different preferences. Presumably, suicide bombers, who have unfortunately become part of the twenty-first-century political landscape, are simply trying to maximize the number of virgins they will meet in heaven.

The problem is that economic theory has little predictive value if preferences are not limited to something like material self-interest, such as the pursuit of income or wealth. If one broadens the notion of utility to include extremes of both selfish and altruistic behavior, one is not saying much more than the tautology that people will pursue whatever it is they pursue. What one really needs is a theory of why some people pursue money and security, while others choose to die for a cause or to give time and money to help other people. To say that Mother Teresa and a Wall Street hedge fund manager are both maximizing their utility misses something important about their motivations.

In practice, most economists indeed assume that utility is based on some form of material self-interest, which will trump other kinds of motivations. This is a view shared by both contemporary free market economists and classical Marxists, the latter of whom maintained that history was shaped by social classes pursuing their economic self-interest. Economics has become a dominant and prestigious social science today because people do much of the time behave according to the economists' more restrictive version of human motivation. Material incentives matter. In Communist China, agricultural productivity on collective farms was low because peasants were not allowed to keep any surplus they produced; they would shirk rather than work hard. A saying in the former Communist world was that "they pretend to pay us and we pretend to work." When incentives were changed in the late 1970s to allow peasants to keep their surplus, agricultural output doubled within four years. One of the causes of the 2008 financial crisis was that investment bankers were rewarded for short-term profits and were not punished when their risky investments blew up a few years later. Fixing the problem would require changing those incentives.

But while the standard economic model does explain a good deal of human behavior, it also has a lot of weaknesses. Over the past couple of decades, behavioral economists and psychologists such as Daniel Kahneman and Amos Tversky have attacked the model's underlying assumptions by showing that people are not rational in practice, that they for example choose default behaviors over more optimal strategies or economize on the hard work of thinking by copying the behavior of others around them.[1]

While behavioral economics has underlined the weaknesses of the existing rational-choice paradigm, it has not posited a clear alternative model of human behavior. In particular, it has not had much to say about the nature of people's underlying preferences. Economic theory does not satisfactorily explain either the soldier falling on the grenade, or the suicide bomber, or a host of other cases where something other than material self-interest appears to be in play. It is hard to say that we "desire" things that are painful, dangerous, or costly in the same way we desire food or money in the bank. So we need to look to other accounts of human behavior that go beyond the economic ones that are so dominant today. This broader understanding has always existed; the problem is that we often forget things we once knew.

Theories of human behavior are built on theories of human nature: regularities that arise out of a universally shared human biology, as opposed to those that are rooted in the norms or customs of the different communities in which people live. The boundary line between nature and nurture is highly contested today, but few people would deny that the two poles of this dichotomy exist. Fortunately, one does not have to establish the boundary precisely in order to develop a theory that gives us useful insight into human motivation.

Early modern thinkers such as Thomas Hobbes, John Locke, and Jean-Jacques Rousseau theorized at length about the "state of nature," a primordial time before the emergence of human society. The state of nature is, however, just a metaphor for human nature; that is, the most basic characteristics of human beings that exist independently of one's particular society or culture. In the Western philosophical tradition, such discussions of human nature go much further back, at least to Plato's *Republic*.

The *Republic* is a dialogue between the philosopher Socrates and two young aristocratic Athenians, Adeimantus and his brother Glaucon, about the nature of a just city. After debunking several existing theories of justice, such as Thrasymachus' assertion that justice is nothing more than the self-interest of the strong, Socrates constructs a just city "in speech," based on an exploration of the nature of the soul. The word *soul* (Greek *psyche*) is not much used anymore, but as the etymology suggests, the discipline of psychology essentially studies the same subject.

The key discussion of the nature of the soul takes place in Book IV. Socrates notes that a desiring part seeks, for example, food and water. But at times a thirsty man pulls back from drinking because he knows the water is tainted and could lead to sickness. Socrates asks, "Isn't there something in their soul bidding them to drink and something forbidding them to do so, something different that masters that which bids?"[2] Adeimantus and Socrates agree that this second, different part of the soul is the calculating part, and that it can operate at cross-purposes from the irrational, desiring part of the soul.

Socrates and Adeimantus have at this point described the modern economic model: the desiring part corresponds to individual preferences, while the calculating part is the rational maximizer. While Sigmund Freud is no longer taken as seriously as he once was, this distinction corresponds roughly to his concept of the desiring id and the ego that kept those desires under control, largely the result of social pressures. But Socrates points to another type of behavior by relating the story of the Athenian Leontius, who passes by a pile of corpses left by the public executioner. Leontius wants to look at the corpses, but at the same time tries to avoid doing so; after an internal struggle, he looks, saying, "Look, you damned wretches, take your fill of the fair sight."[3] Leontius, while tempted to indulge his desire to see the corpses, knew it was ignoble; that he gave in to his cravings aroused his anger and self-loathing. Socrates asks:

And in many other places, don't we . . . notice that, when desire forces someone contrary to the calculating part, he reproaches himself and his spirit is roused against that in him which is doing the forcing; and, just as though there were two parties at faction, such a man's spirit becomes the ally of speech?[4]

We could transpose this into a more contemporary example, where a drug addict or alcoholic knows that another hit or drink is bad for him or her, but nonetheless takes it and feels a deep self-loathing for being weak. Socrates uses a new word, *spirit*, to refer to the part of the soul that is the seat of this anger against oneself, which is a poor translation of the Greek word *thymos*.

Socrates then asks Adeimantus whether the part of the soul that wanted not to look at the corpses was just another desire or was an aspect of the calculating part, since they both pushed in the same direction. The former view would be the perspective of contemporary economics, where one desire is limited only by the calculation that another, more important desire supersedes it. Socrates asks, is there a third part of the soul?

What we are now bringing to light about the spirited is the opposite of our recent assertion. Then we supposed it had something to do with the desiring part; but now, far from it, we say that in the faction of the soul it sets its arms on the side of the calculating part.

Quite so, [Adeimantus] said.

Is it then different from the calculating part as well, or is it a particular form of it so that there aren't three forms in the soul but two, the calculating part and the desiring? Or just as there were three classes in the city that held it together, money-making, auxiliary, and deliberative, is there in the soul too this third, the spirited, by nature an auxiliary to the calculating part, if not corrupted by bad rearing?[5]

Adeimantus immediately agrees with Socrates that the spirited part—thymos—is neither just another desire nor an aspect of reason but an independent part of the soul. Thymos is the seat of both anger and pride: Leontius was proud and believed he had a better self that would resist looking at the corpses, and when he gave in to his desires, he became angry at his failure to live up to that standard.

More than two millennia before its advent, Socrates and Adeimantus understood something unrecognized by modern economics. Desire and reason are component parts of the human psyche (soul), but a third part, thymos, acts completely independently of the first two. Thymos is the seat of judgments of worth: Leontius believed he was above staring at corpses, just as a drug addict wants to be a productive employee or a loving mother. Human beings do not just want things that are external to themselves, such as food, drink, Lamborghinis, or that next hit. They also crave positive judgments about their worth or dignity. Those judgments can come from within, as in Leontius' case, but they are most often made by other people in the society around them who *recognize* their worth. If they receive that positive judgment, they feel pride, and if they do not receive it, they feel either anger (when they think they are being undervalued) or shame (when they realize that they have not lived up to other people's standards).

This third part of the soul, thymos, is the seat of today's identity politics. Political actors do struggle over economic issues: whether taxes should be lower or higher, or how the pie of government revenue will be divided among different claimants in a democracy. But a lot of political life is only weakly related to economic resources.

Take, for example, the gay marriage movement, which has spread like wildfire across the developed world in the first decades of the twenty-first century. This does have an economic aspect, having to do with rights of survivorship, inheritance, and the like for gay or lesbian unions. However, many of those economic issues could have been and were in many cases resolved through new rules about property in civil unions. But a civil union would have had lower status than a marriage: society would be saying that gay people could be together legally, but their bond would be different from that between a man and a woman. This outcome was unacceptable to millions of people who wanted their political systems to explicitly *recognize* the equal dignity of gays and lesbians; the ability to marry was just a marker of that equal dignity. And those opposed wanted something of the opposite: a clear affirmation of the superior dignity of a heterosexual union and therefore of the traditional family. The emotions expended over gay marriage had much more to do with assertions about dignity than they did with economics.

Similarly, the massive anger of women embodied in the #MeToo movement that emerged in the wake of revelations about the behavior of Hollywood producer Harvey Weinstein was fundamentally about respect. While the way in which powerful men had coerced vulnerable women had an economic dimension, the wrong of valuing a woman for her sexuality or looks alone and not for other characteristics such as competence or character would exist among men and women of equal wealth or power.

But we are getting ahead of ourselves in the story of thymos and identity. Socrates in the *Republic* does not argue that thymos is a characteristic shared equally among all human beings, nor does he suggest that it makes itself manifest in a variety of forms. It appears as something associated with a particular class of human beings in his imaginary city, the guardians or auxiliaries who would be responsible for defending the city from its enemies. They are warriors, different from shopkeepers, for whom desires and their satisfaction are the chief characteristic, as well as from the deliberative class of leaders, who use their reason to determine what is best for the city. Socrates suggests that the thymotic guardians are typically angry and compares them to dogs who are vicious toward strangers and loyal to their masters. As warriors they must be courageous; they must be willing to risk their lives and undergo hardship in a way that neither the merchant class nor the deliberative class would. Anger and pride rather than reason or desire motivates them to take the risks they do.

In speaking this way, Socrates reflects the reality of the classical world, indeed, the reality of most civilizations around the world that possessed an aristocratic class whose claim to high social status lay in the fact that they, or their ancestors, were warriors. The Greek word for "gentleman" was *kaloskagathos*, or "beautiful and good," while the very word *aristocracy* derives from the Greek term "rule by the best." These warriors were seen as morally different from shopkeepers because of their virtue: they were willing to risk their lives for the public good. Honor accrued only to people who deliberately rejected rational utility maximization—our modern economic model—in favor of those who were willing to risk the most important utility of all, their lives.

Today, we tend to look back on aristocrats with a great deal of cynicism, regarding them at best as self-important parasites, and at worst as violent predators on the rest of their society. Their descendants are even worse, since they did not themselves earn the status that their families receive, but got it as an accident of birth. We have to recognize, however, that in aristocratic societies there was a deeply rooted belief that honor or esteem was not due to everyone, but only to the class of people who risked their lives. An echo of that feeling still exists in the respect we citizens of modern democratic societies typically pay to soldiers who die for their country, or policemen and firemen who risk their lives in the line of duty. Dignity or esteem is not due to everyone, least of all to businesspeople or workers whose main objective is to maximize their own welfare. Aristocrats thought of themselves as better than other people and possessed what we may call megalothymia, the desire to be recognized as superior. Predemocratic societies rested on a foundation of social hierarchy, so this belief in the inherent superiority of a certain class of people was fundamental to the maintenance of social order.

The problem with megalothymia is that for every person recognized as superior, far more people are seen as inferior and do not receive any public recognition of their human worth. While Socrates and Adeimantus associate thymos primarily with the class of guardians, they also seem to think that all human beings possess all three parts of the soul. Nonguardians have their pride as well, a pride that is injured when the nobleman slaps them in the face and orders them out of the way, or when a daughter or a wife is taken involuntarily as sexual plaything by her social "betters." While a certain group of humans always want to be seen as superior, a powerful feeling of resentment arises when one is disrespected. Moreover, while we are willing to laud people with certain kinds of achievement, such as the great athlete or musician, many social honors are rooted not in true superiority, but rather in social convention. We can easily resent people who are recognized for the wrong things, such as exhibitionist socialites or reality-show stars who are no better than us.

So an equally powerful human drive is to be seen as "just as good" as everyone else, something we may label "isothymia."[6] Megalothymia is what economist Robert Frank labels a "positional good"—something that by its very nature cannot be shared because it is based on one's position relative to someone else.[7] The rise of modern democracy is the story of the displacement of megalothymia by isothymia: societies that only recognized an elite few were replaced by ones that recognized everyone as inherently equal. In Europe, societies stratified by class began to recognize the rights of ordinary people, and nations that had been submerged in great empires sought a separate and equal status. The great struggles in American political history—over slavery and segregation, workers' rights, women's equality—were ultimately demands that the political system expand the circle of individuals it recognized as having equal rights.

Yet the story is more complicated than that. Contemporary identity politics is driven by the quest for equal recognition by groups that have been marginalized by their societies. But that desire for equal recognition can easily slide over into a demand for recognition of the group's superiority. This is a large part of the story of nationalism and national identity, as well as certain forms of extremist religious politics today.

A further problem with isothymia is that certain human activities will inevitably entail greater respect than others. To deny this is to deny the possibility of human excellences. I cannot play the piano and cannot pretend that I am the equal of

Glenn Gould or Arthur Rubinstein in this regard. No community will fail to pay greater honor to the soldier or police officer who risks his or her life for the common good than to the coward who flees at the first sign of danger or, worse yet, betrays the community to outsiders. Recognition of everyone's equal worth means a failure to recognize the worth of people who are actually superior in some sense.

Isothymia demands that we recognize the basic equal worth of our fellow human beings. In democratic societies we assert, with the American Declaration of Independence, that "all men are created equal." Yet historically, we have disagreed on who qualifies as "all men." At the time that the declaration was signed, this circle did not include white men without property, black slaves, indigenous Americans, or women. Moreover, since human beings are so obviously varied in their talents and capacities, we need to understand in what sense we are willing to recognize them as equal for political purposes. The Declaration of Independence says this is "self-evident," without giving us much guidance on how we are to understand equality.

Thymos is the part of the soul that seeks recognition. In the *Republic*, only a narrow class of people sought recognition of their dignity, on the basis of their willingness to risk their lives as warriors. Yet the desire for recognition also seems to lie within every human soul. The shopkeepers or artisans or beggars on the street can also feel the pang of disrespect. But that feeling is inchoate, and they do not have a clear sense of why they should be respected. Their society is telling them that they are not worth as much as the aristocrat; why not accept society's judgment? For much of human history, this was indeed the fate of the great mass of humanity.

But while thymos is a universal aspect of human nature that has always existed, the belief that each of us has an inner self that is worthy of respect, and that the surrounding society may be wrong in not recognizing it, is a more recent phenomenon. So while the concept of identity is rooted in thymos, it emerged only in modern times when it was combined with a notion of an inner and an outer self, and the radical view that the inner self was more valuable than the outer one. This was the product of both a shift in ideas about the self and the realities of societies that started to evolve rapidly under the pressures of economic and technological change.

3

INSIDE AND OUTSIDE

Unlike thymos, which is a permanent part of human nature, what was to become the modern concept of identity emerged only as societies started to modernize a few hundred years ago. While it originated in Europe, it has subsequently spread and taken root in virtually all societies around the globe.

The foundations of identity were laid with the perception of a disjunction between one's inside and one's outside. Individuals come to believe that they have a true or authentic identity hiding within themselves that is somehow at odds with the role they are assigned by their surrounding society. The modern concept of identity places a supreme value on authenticity, on the validation of that inner being that is not being allowed to express itself. It is on the side of the inner and not the outer self. Oftentimes an individual may not understand who that inner self really is, but has only the vague feeling that he or she is being forced to live a lie. This can lead to an obsessive focus on the question "Who am I, really?" The search for an answer produces feelings of alienation and anxiety and can only be relieved when one accepts that inner self and receives public recognition for it. And if that outer society is going to properly recognize the inner self, one has to imagine society itself being able to change in fundamental ways.

In the West, the idea of identity was born, in a sense, during the Protestant Reformation, and it was given its initial expression by the Augustinian friar Martin Luther. Luther received a traditional theological education and a professorship at Wittenberg; for ten years, he read, thought, and struggled with his inner self. In the words of one historian, Luther "found himself in a state of despair before God. He wanted the assurance of being acceptable to God, but could discover in himself only the certainty of sin and in God only an inexorable justice which condemned to futility all his efforts at repentance and his search for the divine mercy."[1] Luther sought the remedies of mortification recommended by the Catholic Church, before realizing that he could do nothing to bribe, cajole, or entreat God. He understood that the Church acted only on the outer person—through confession, penance, alms, worship of saints— none of which could make a difference because grace was bestowed only as a free act of love by God.

Luther was one of the first Western thinkers to articulate and valorize the inner self over the external social being. He argued that man has a twofold nature, an inner spiritual one and an outer bodily being; since "no external thing has any influence in producing Christian righteousness or freedom," only the inner man could be renewed.

Faith alone can rule only in the inner man, as Romans 10[:10] says, "For man believes with his heart and so is justified," and since faith alone justifies, it is clear that the inner man cannot be justified, freed, or saved by any outer work or action at all, and that these works, whatever their character, have nothing to do with this inner man.[2]

This recognition—central to subsequent Protestant doctrine—that faith alone and not works would justify man in one stroke undercut the raison d'être for the Catholic Church. The Church was an intermediary between man and God, but it could shape only the outer man through its rituals and works. Luther was horrified by the decadence and corruption of the medieval Church, but the more profound insight was that the Church itself was unnecessary and, indeed, blasphemous in its efforts to coerce or bribe God. Luther himself would not be the teenager brought back to obedience by society; rather, society itself would have to adjust to the demands of the inner person. Though it was not Luther's intention, the Reformation brought about exactly this result: the decline of Rome as the Universal Church, the rise of alternative churches, and a whole series of social changes in which the individual believer was prioritized over prevailing social structures.

Social theorists have long debated whether the monumental changes that took place in Europe following the Reformation—what we call modernization—were the product of material forces or were driven by ideas such as those of Luther. Karl Marx and contemporary neoclassical economists would say that Luther's ideas were derivative of the material conditions: had there not been widespread economic discontents and divisions among the German princes, his views would never have spread the way they did. On the other hand, the sociologist Max Weber argued for the primacy of ideas: the very material conditions that economists study could only come about because they were legitimated by changes in the way people thought about them; similar conditions in previous times did not produce the same results because the intellectual climate was different.

In my view, both positions capture part of the truth, because causality moves in both directions at once. Material conditions obviously shape people's receptivity to certain ideas. But ideas have their own inner logic, and without the cognitive framing they provide, people will interpret their material conditions differently. This affects our understanding of the evolution of the concept of identity, since it was driven by both an evolution in thought and the changing conditions of the broader society as Europe began the process of socioeconomic modernization.

On the plane of ideas, we can see that the distinction between inner and outer, and the valorization of the former over the latter, starts in an important sense with Luther.* Like many subsequent thinkers struggling with the question of identity, he began with an agonizing quest to understand himself, and the way in which he might be justified before God. This inner man was not good; he was a sinner, but could yet be saved through an inner act of belief that could not be made visible by any external action. Thus Luther is responsible for the notion, central to questions of identity, that the inner self is deep and possesses many layers that can be exposed only through private introspection.

Yet Martin Luther stands far from more modern understandings of identity. He celebrated the freedom of the inner

---

* Many centuries before Martin Luther, Augustine went through a similar tortured exploration of his inner self in his *Confessions*. Unlike Luther, however, his writings did not devalue established social institutions or trigger massive upheavals in the politics and society of his time.

self, but that self had only one dimension: faith, and the acceptance of God's grace. It was a binary choice: one was free to choose God, or not. One could not choose to be a Hindu or a Buddhist or decide that one's true identity lay in coming out of the closet as gay or lesbian. Luther was not facing a "crisis of meaning," something that would have been incomprehensible to him; while he rejected the Universal Church, he accepted completely the underlying truth of Christianity.[3]

The second sense in which Luther had not yet arrived at the modern understanding of identity was that his inner self did not seek public recognition of its newfound freedom. Indeed, he agonized over his own motives: he sought to avoid the taint of self-satisfaction, knowing "himself to be an incorrigible sinner, incapable of escaping what he called concupiscence (the sin of doing the right thing not merely to please God but with an eye to self)."[4] While he received enormous recognition in his lifetime and was capable of monumental bouts of righteous anger, his doctrine of faith was built on the private relationship of man to God and not on any form of public approval.

Nonetheless, the distinction between inner and outer had been established and could be filled with new forms of inner freedom by subsequent thinkers who did not accept Martin Luther's Christian worldview.

By the late eighteenth century, the idea at the core of modern identity had evolved much further and now took on a secular form. The Canadian political theorist Charles Taylor has written the definitive account of this process, and in it, the philosopher Jean-Jacques Rousseau plays a central role.[5] Rousseau was the fundamental source of many ideas that would later be critical to a host of modern trends: democracy, human rights, communism, the discipline of anthropology, and environmentalism. For him, however, the natural goodness of the inner self was a theme that tied together his varied political, social, and personal writings.[6]

Rousseau reversed the Christian moral evaluation of the inner human being. Christians such as Luther believed in original sin: human beings were fallen creatures who could be redeemed only through God's love. In his *Discourse on the Origins of Inequality*, Rousseau argued that the first human being—man in the state of nature—was *not* sinful. The characteristics we associate with sin and evil—jealousy, greed, violence, hatred, and the like—did not characterize the earliest humans. In Rousseau's account, there was no original human society: early people were fearful, isolated creatures with limited needs, for whom sex but not the family was natural. They did not feel greed or envy; their only natural emotion was pity for the suffering of others.

According to Rousseau, human unhappiness begins with the discovery of society. The first humans began their descent into society by mastering animals, which "produced the first movement of pride in him." They then started to cooperate for mutual protection and advantage; this closer association "engendered in the mind of man perceptions of certain relations . . . which we express by the words great, little, strong, weak, swift, slow, fearful, bold, and other similar ideas." The ability to compare, and to evaluate, other human beings was the fountainhead of human unhappiness: "Men no sooner began to set a value upon each other, and know what esteem was, than each laid claim to it, and it was no longer safe for any man to refuse it to another." Rousseau denounces the shift from *amour de soi* (love of self) to *amour propre* (self-love or vanity); simple self-interest is transmuted into feelings of pride and the desire for social recognition.[7]

Rousseau says that private property emerged with the discovery of metallurgy and agriculture; while making humans incomparably richer, the ability to accumulate property also vastly exaggerated natural differences between individuals and raised jealousy, envy, pride, and shame to new heights. Hence Rousseau's famous injunction at the beginning of the second part of the *Discourse*:

> The first person who, having enclosed some land, took it upon himself to say "This is mine," and found people simple-minded enough to believe him, was the true founder of civil society . . . How many crimes, wars, murders, miseries and horrors, would that man have saved the human species, who pulling up the stakes or filling up the ditches should have cried to his fellows: Don't listen to this imposter; you are lost, if you forget that the fruits of the earth belong equally to us all, and the earth to nobody![8]

Rousseau had two separate prescriptions for walking mankind back out of this catastrophe of inequality and violence. The first was outlined in *The Social Contract*, a political solution in which citizens return to their natural equality through the emergence of a "general will" that unites them in republican virtue. They cooperate with one another in a political union, but one that brooks no disagreement or pluralism. This solution has been rightly criticized as proto-totalitarian, quashing diversity and requiring strict uniformity of thought.

The second prescription is not political but plays out on an individual level. In his late work *Reveries of a Solitary Walker*, Rousseau tries to recover the state of consciousness of the first man—that is, humans as they were prior to the discovery of society. In the *Discourse on Inequality*, he had said that "the first sentiment of Man was that of his existence"; the *sentiment de l'existence* returns in the *Reveries* as a feeling of plenitude and happiness that emerges as an individual seeks to uncover the true self hiding beneath the layers of acquired social sensibilities.[9] Rousseau's sentiment of existence would one day morph into what is now called lived experience, which lies at the root of contemporary identity politics.

Rousseau thus stakes out a distinctive position regarding human nature. He disputes the assertion of Thomas Hobbes that man in the state of nature was violent, cruel, and selfish; Rousseau also disagrees with John Locke that private property was natural to early man. He would also disagree with Socrates and Adeimantus that thymos was a constituent part of the human soul, since Rousseau asserts clearly that the emotion of pride, and hence the desire to be recognized by other people, did not exist for the earliest human beings.

What Rousseau asserts, and what becomes foundational in world politics in the subsequent centuries, is that a thing called society exists outside the individual, a mass of rules, relationships, injunctions, and customs that is itself the chief obstacle to the realization of human potential, and hence of human happiness. This way of thinking has become so instinctive to us now that we are unconscious of it. It is evident in the case of the teenager accused of a crime who raises the defense "Society made me do it," or of the woman who feels that her potential is being limited by the gendered and sexist society around her. On a larger scale, it is evident in the complaints of a Vladimir Putin who feels the American-led international order wrongly disrespects Russia, and who then seeks to overturn it. While earlier thinkers could critique aspects of existing social rules and customs, few argued that existing society and its rules needed to be abolished en masse and replaced by something better. This is what ultimately links Rousseau to the revolutionary politics of France in 1789, or Russia in 1917, or China in 1949.

Like Luther, Rousseau establishes a sharp distinction between the inner self and the outer society demanding conformity to its rules. Unlike Luther, however, the freedom of that inner individual does not lie only in his or her ability to accept the grace of God; rather, it lies in the natural and universal ability to experience the *sentiment de l'existence*, free of the layers of accumulated social convention. Rousseau thus secularized and generalized the interiority opened up by Luther, accomplished through an exploration of Rousseau's innermost feelings that was as anguished and prolonged as that of the Augustinian friar. According to Charles Taylor, "This is part of the massive subjective turn of modern culture, a new form of inwardness, in which we come to think of ourselves as beings with inner depths."[10]

Rousseau's secularization of the inner self, and the priority he gives it over social convention, is thus a critical stepping-stone to the modern idea of identity. But Rousseau, as we have seen, did not believe that the desire for recognition was natural to human beings. He argued that the emotion of pride and the proclivity to compare oneself to others did not exist among early human beings, and that their emergence in human history laid the foundation for subsequent human unhappiness. The recovery of the inner self thus required divesting oneself of the need for social recognition; the solitary dreamer does not need anyone's approval.

We might note how, given our present knowledge of early human societies and of human evolution, Rousseau was profoundly right about certain things, and profoundly wrong about others. He was largely correct in his description of the broad stages of human social evolution, tracing the transitions from what we would now call hunter-gatherer to agrarian and then to commercial societies. He was also correct in his emphasis on the importance of the discovery of agriculture: how it led to the institution of private property, and to agrarian societies that were far more unequal and hierarchical than the hunter-gatherer ones they displaced.[11]

But Rousseau was wrong about some important things, beginning with his assertion that early humans were primordially individualistic. We know he was wrong, first because we see no archaeological or anthropological evidence of presocial human beings, and second because we know with high confidence that the primate ancestors of modern human beings were themselves highly social. Existing primates have complex social structures along with, evidently, the emotional faculties needed to sustain them.[12] Rousseau's assertion that pride emerged only at a certain stage of social evolution is curious; it begs the question of how such an intrinsic human feeling could spontaneously appear in response to an external stimulus. If pride were socially constructed, young children would have to be somehow trained to experience it, yet we do not observe this happening to our children. Today we know that feelings of pride and self-esteem are related to levels of the neurotransmitter serotonin in the brain, and that chimpanzees exhibit elevated levels of serotonin when they achieve alpha male status.[13] It seems unlikely that there was ever a moment when behaviorally modern human beings did not compare themselves with one another or feel pride when they received social recognition. In this respect, Plato had a better understanding of human nature than Rousseau.

That the distinction between an inner and an outer self emerged in Europe between the Reformation and the French Revolution was not an accident. European society was undergoing a series of profound economic and social changes that created the material conditions by which such ideas could spread.

All human societies socialize their members to live by common rules; human cooperation, and hence human success as a species, would not be possible otherwise. All societies have had rebellious teenagers and misfits who didn't want to accept those rules, but in this struggle, society almost always wins out by forcing inner selves to conform to external norms.

Hence the concept of identity as it is now understood would not even arise in most traditional human societies. For much of the last ten thousand years of human history, the vast majority of people lived in settled agrarian communities. In such societies, social roles are both limited and fixed: a strict hierarchy is based on age and gender; everyone has the same occupation (farming or raising children and minding a household); one's entire life is lived in the same small village with a limited circle of friends and neighbors; one's religion and beliefs are shared by all; and social mobility—moving away from the village, choosing a different occupation, or marrying someone not chosen by one's parents—is virtually impossible. Such societies have neither pluralism, nor diversity, nor choice. Given this lack of choice, it did not make sense for an individual to sit around and brood over the question "Who am I, really?" All of the characteristics that make up an inner self are fixed. One could perhaps rebel by running away to another village, but there one would find oneself trapped in an identical limited social space. There was no concept of "society" standing outside the individual, limiting a person's choices, and no valorization of an inner self over that society.

All of this began to change as a broad modernization took hold in Europe. A commercial revolution was unfolding that vastly expanded trade and began to upend established social hierarchies. Adam Smith argued in *The Wealth of Nations* that "the division of labour is limited by the extent of the market"; as markets grew through technological change, new occupations appeared and different social classes emerged. Cities were growing in power and independence, cities that served as havens for peasants seeking to escape the tyranny of their lords. The Reformation set off a century and a half of religious warfare that scrambled the political map of Europe. It opened up possibilities for religious choice in ways that had not been possible under the medieval Church. Invention of the printing press led to the spread of literacy and the rapid diffusion of new ideas.

These broader social and economic changes meant that individuals suddenly had more choice and opportunity in their lives. In the old society, their limited social choices determined who they were on the inside; with new horizons opening up, the question "Who am I?" suddenly became more relevant, as did perceptions of a vast gulf that existed between the inner person and external reality. Ideas shaped the material world, and the material world created conditions for the spread of certain ideas.

4

FROM DIGNITY TO DEMOCRACY

The modern concept of identity unites three different phenomena. The first is thymos, a universal aspect of human personality that craves recognition. The second is the distinction between the inner and the outer self, and the raising of the moral valuation of the inner self over outer society. This emerged only in early modern Europe. The third is an evolving concept of dignity, in which recognition is due not just to a narrow class of people, but to everyone. The broadening and universalization of dignity turns the private quest for self into a political project. In Western political thought, this shift took place in the generation after Rousseau, through the philosophers Immanuel Kant and particularly Georg Wilhelm Friedrich Hegel.

According to Socrates, dignity was demanded primarily by the political community's warriors who exhibited courage and were willing to risk death in public service. That is one understanding of human dignity, but there are others. In the Bible's book of Genesis, Adam and Eve exist in a state of innocence until the serpent tempts Eve with a fruit from the Tree of the Knowledge of Good and Evil. Upon eating the fruit, they immediately see their nakedness and are ashamed of it and try to cover it up. God banishes them from the Garden of Eden for this transgression of his commandment, and the human race thereafter lives in the fallen condition proceeding from this original sin.

The Christian concept of dignity has revolved around this capacity for moral choice. Human beings are able to distinguish between good and evil; they can choose to do good, even if they often, like Adam and Eve, do not do so. Luther's justification by faith was simply an expression of this choice. And though Adam and Eve made the wrong choice, their choice would be meaningless if they were not capable of sinning. By eating the fruit, they established their moral status and that of their descendants, who would henceforth know the difference between good and evil and be able to choose. Animals are incapable of knowing good and evil since they operate on instinct, while God in a sense is pure goodness and always chooses rightly. The human capacity for choice gives people a higher status than that of animals since it partakes of God's capacity for goodness, yet is less than that of God since people are capable of sin. In this sense, in the Christian tradition, all human beings are fundamentally equal: they are all endowed with an equal capacity for choice. The centrality of moral choice to human dignity was underlined by the Baptist minister Martin Luther King, Jr., when he said, "I have a dream that my four little children will one day live in a nation where they will not be judged by the color of their skin but by the content of their character"—i.e., by the moral choices made by their inner selves, and not by their external characteristics.

Immanuel Kant presented a secular version of this Christian understanding of dignity in his *Critique of Practical Reason* and other writings such as his *Groundwork to a Metaphysics of Morals*. He asserts that we can point to nothing as unconditionally good other than a good will—that is, the capacity for proper moral choice. But Kant did not see this in religious terms; moral choice for him consists of the ability to follow abstract rules of reason for their own sake, and not for instrumental reasons having to do with the outcomes such choices imply for human well-being or happiness. The human capacity for moral choice means that human beings are not machines subject to the laws of physics, as Hobbes suggested; they are moral agents who can choose independently of their material environment and, for that reason, need to be treated not as ends to other means, but as ends in themselves. Morality is not a utilitarian calculus of outcomes that maximize human happiness, but about the act of choice itself. For Kant, human dignity revolves around human will, that human beings are genuine agents or uncaused causes.

The philosopher Hegel accepted this link between moral choice and human dignity; human beings are morally free agents who are not simply rational machines seeking to maximize satisfaction of their desires. But unlike Rousseau or Kant, Hegel put recognition of that moral agency at the center of his account of the human condition. In *The Phenomenology of Spirit*, he argued that human history was driven by a struggle for recognition. The demand comes initially from a warrior who is willing to risk his life in a bloody battle, not for territory or wealth, but simply for recognition itself. But this recognition ultimately fails to be satisfying because it is the recognition of a slave, that is, of someone without dignity. This problem can be solved only when the slave acquires dignity through labor, through the ability to transform the world into a place suitable for human life. The only rational form of recognition is ulti-mately the mutual recognition of master and slave of their shared human dignity.

These struggles for Hegel do not play themselves out primarily as individual journeys into the self, as they did for Rousseau, but politically. The great conflict of his day was the French Revolution, and its enshrining of the Rights of Man. The young Hegel witnessed Napoleon riding through his university town after the Battle of Jena in 1806 and saw in that act the incipient universalization of recognition in the form of the principles of the French Revolution. This is the sense in which Hegel believed that history had come to an end: it culminated in the idea of universal recognition; subsequent events would simply carry this principle to the far corners of the earth.[1]

A liberal democratic regime based on individual rights enshrines the notion of equal dignity in law by recognizing citizens as moral agents capable of sharing in their own self-government. In Hegel's day, this principle was being imposed on countries by a general on horseback, but for the philosopher this was a small detail in the larger story of the growth of human freedom.

By the early nineteenth century, most of the elements of the modern concept of identity are present: the distinction between the inner and the outer selves, the valuation of the inner being above existing social arrangements, the understanding that the dignity of the inner self rests on its moral freedom, the view that all human beings share this moral freedom, and the de-mand that the free inner self be recognized. Hegel pointed to a fundamental truth about modern politics, that the great pas-sions unleashed by events such as the French Revolution were at base struggles over dignity. The inner self was not just a matter of personal reflection; its freedom was to be embodied in rights and law. The democratic upsurge that would unfold in the two centuries after the French Revolution was driven by peoples demanding recognition of their political personhood, that they were moral agents capable of sharing in political power.

The slaves would, in other words, rebel against the masters; a world in which the dignity of only a few was recognized would be replaced by one whose founding principle would be recognition of the dignity of all.

5

REVOLUTIONS OF DIGNITY

The demand for the equal recognition of dignity animated the French Revolution, and it continues to the present day.

On December 17, 2010, police confiscated the produce from the vegetable cart of a Tunisian street vendor named Mohamed Bouazizi, ostensibly because he did not have a permit. According to his family, he was publicly slapped by a policewoman, Faida Hamdi, who confiscated his electronic scales as well and spat in his face. (That Hamdi was female may have increased his feeling of humiliation in a male-dominated culture.) Bouazizi went to the governor's office to complain and to get his scales back, but the governor refused to see him. Bouazizi then doused himself in gasoline and set himself on fire, shouting, "How do you expect me to make a living?"

News of this incident spread like wildfire throughout the Arab world, triggering what became known as the Arab Spring. The immediate effect was felt in Tunisia, where less than a month later widespread rioting led to the resignation and departure of the country's long-standing dictator, Zine El Abidine Ben Ali. Massive protests broke out in other Arab cities, most notably in nearby Egypt, where that country's strongman, Hosni Mubarak, was driven from power in February 2011. Protests and uprisings took place in Libya, Yemen, Bahrain, and Syria, as populations felt empowered and were suddenly willing to criticize authoritarian leaders. What was shared among all of these protesters was resentment that they had been humiliated and disregarded by their governments.

In subsequent years, the Arab Spring went horribly wrong. The greatest tragedy occurred in Syria, where that country's dictator, Bashar al-Assad, refused to leave power and launched a war against his own population that has to date killed more than 400,000 people and displaced millions more. In Egypt, early democratic elections brought the Muslim Brotherhood to power; fears that they would impose their brand of Islam on the country led the military to stage a coup in 2013. Libya and Yemen have descended into bloody civil wars, and authoritarian rulers tightened their grip throughout the region. Only Tunisia, where the Arab Spring originated, looks anything like a liberal democracy, but it is hanging on by a thread.

It is easy to look back on these events and argue that the Arab Spring from the beginning had nothing to do with democracy, and that the dominant political trend in the region is an intolerant form of Islamism. Yet this doesn't do justice to the political passions that were unleashed by Mohamed Bouazizi's self-immolation. The Arab world had been suffering under repressive and stagnant dictatorships for years; why all of a sudden did masses of people risk their lives in response to a single incident?

The particulars of Bouazizi's story are critical. He was not a protester or a political prisoner mistreated by the regime, but an ordinary citizen who was struggling to make a living in the informal economy. Many entrepreneurs in the developing world remain informal because governments make it too difficult to comply with a host of legal requirements to run a formal business. What made Bouazizi's experience all too familiar to millions of people in the Arab world was the way that he was treated by the Tunisian state: the goods on which his living depended were arbitrarily confiscated, he was publicly humiliated, and when he tried to complain and receive justice, no one would listen. The state was not treating him like a *human being*: that is, a moral agent worthy of a minimum amount of respect, who would at least have deserved an explanation or justification for why his livelihood had been seized. For millions of people in the Arab world, his self-immolation crystallized the sense of injustice they felt toward the regimes they were living under.

The Arab world subsequently fell into chaos because the Arabs themselves could not agree on what type of regime would replace the old dictatorships. Yet for a moment in 2011 they had a strong consensus on what they didn't like: authoritarian governments that treated them at best as children, and at worst as subjects to be cheated by corrupt politicians, exploited economically, or used as cannon fodder in wars.

Over the past two generations, the world has seen a large number of spontaneous uprisings against authoritarian governments, from the protests that brought down Communist regimes in 1989, to the South African transition from apartheid, to other citizen mobilizations in sub-Saharan Africa in the 1990s, to the "color revolutions" in Georgia and Ukraine in the early 2000s in which recognition of basic human dignity was a central issue.

One of those uprisings, indeed, came to be known as the

Revolution of Dignity. In November 2013 Ukrainian president Viktor Yanukovych announced that he was suspending his country's attempt to finalize an association agreement with the European Union and would seek instead closer cooperation with Russia and Russian president Vladimir Putin's Eurasian Economic Union. Yanukovych had been president at the time of the Orange Revolution in 2004; his effort to rig his reelection triggered a popular uprising that drove him from power. Yet by 2010 he had returned to the presidency as the corrupt and squabbling Orange Coalition that came to power failed to deliver on its promises.

Yanukovych's effort to take Ukraine back into the Russian orbit triggered a series of spontaneous protests in the capital city, Kyiv, where by early December nearly 800,000 people had gathered in Maidan to support continued alignment with the EU. The regime responded with violence, but as in many situations of this sort, the killing of protesters simply fueled the level of outrage and increased the size of the crowds supporting the Euromaidan movement. Following the deaths of more than a hundred protesters in February, Yanukovych lost control of the situation and left the presidency for a second time, leading to a new political opening for Ukraine.

Since these events, Ukraine no more than Tunisia has become a successful liberal democracy. Its economy and politics are dominated by a small group of oligarchs, one of whom, Petro Poroshenko, was elected president later in 2014. The government, while democratically elected, is rife with corruption and has been under attack by neighboring Russia, which seized Crimea that same year and started a war in eastern Ukraine. Yet it is important to understand the underlying motives of the political actors who brought about Euromaidan and the Revolution of Dignity.

The uprising was not about democracy, strictly speaking, if by democracy we mean public choice expressed through elections. Yanukovych had been legitimately elected president in 2010, based on support from his Party of Regions. Rather, the fight was over corruption and abuse of power. Yanukovych as president had been able to accumulate billions of dollars of personal wealth, as revelations about his gaudy palace and other holdings were soon to reveal. The Party of Regions received strong support from a shadowy oligarch, Rinat Akhmetov, who controlled most of the large industries in eastern Ukraine. The choice between aligning with the EU or with Putin's Russia was seen as a choice between living under a modern government that treated people equally qua citizen and living under a regime in which democracy was manipulated by self-dealing kleptocrats behind a veneer of democratic practice. Putin's Russia represented the epitome of this kind of mafia state; closer association with it rather than Europe represented a step into a world in which real power was held by an unaccountable elite. Hence the belief that the Euromaidan uprising was about securing the basic dignity of ordinary citizens.

The impulses evident in the early stages of the Arab Spring and in the color revolutions point to what is the moral core of modern liberal democracy. Such regimes are based on the twin principles of freedom and equality. Freedom can be understood in a negative sense, as freedom from government power. This is the way that many American conservatives interpret the word: individuals should be allowed to get on with their private lives as they see fit. But freedom typically means more than being left alone by the government: it means human agency, the ability to exercise a share of power through active participation in self-government. This was the sense of agency felt by the crowds in the streets of Tunis or Cairo or Kyiv, who for the first time felt that they could change the way that government power was being used. This freedom is institutionalized in the franchise, which gives every citizen a small share of political power. It is also institutionalized in the rights to free speech and free assembly, which are avenues for political self-expression. Many modern democratic constitutions thus enshrine the principle of equal dignity. They are drawing on the Christian tradition that sees dignity rooted in human moral agency. But that agency is no longer seen in a religious sense, as the ability to accept God; rather, it is the ability to share in the exercise of power as a member of a democratic political community.

In modern liberal democracies, the second principle, equality, has seldom been understood to imply a commitment to substantive economic or social equality. Those socialist regimes that tried to make this a reality soon found themselves running afoul of the first principle of freedom, requiring as they did massive state control over their citizens' lives. Market economies depend on the individual pursuit of self-interest, which leads to inequalities of wealth, given people's differing abilities and their conditions of birth. Equality in a modern liberal democracy has always meant something more like an equality of freedom. This means both an equal negative freedom from abusive government power and an equal positive freedom to participate in self-government and economic exchange.

Modern liberal democracies institutionalize these principles of freedom and equality by creating capable states that are nonetheless constrained by a rule of law and democratic accountability. The rule of law limits power by granting citizens certain basic rights—that is, in certain domains such as speech, association, property, and religious belief the state may not restrict individual choice. Rule of law also serves the principle of equality by applying those rules equally to all citizens, including those who hold the highest political offices within the system. Democratic accountability in turn seeks to give all adult citizens an equal share of power by enfranchising them, and allowing them to replace their rulers if they object to their use of power. This is why the rule of law and democratic accountability have typically been tightly intertwined. The law protects both the negative freedom from government abuse and the positive freedom of equal participation, as it did during the civil rights era in the United States. Democratic participation for its part shields the judicial system from abuse. During the English Civil War in the seventeenth century, Parliament rallied to protect the independence of courts, as Polish civil society sought to do in the year 2017, when judicial independence was threatened by the ruling party.

Real-world liberal democracies never fully live up to their underlying ideals of freedom and equality. Rights are often violated; the law never applies equally to the rich and powerful as it does to the poor and weak; citizens, though given the opportunity to participate, frequently choose not to do so. Moreover, intrinsic conflicts exist between the goals of freedom and equality: greater freedom often entails increased inequality, while efforts to equalize outcomes reduce freedom. Successful democracy depends not on optimization of its ideals, but balance: a balance between individual freedom and political equality, and between a capable state exercising legitimate power and the institutions of law and accountability that seek to constrain it. Many democracies try to do a whole lot more than this, through policies that try to promote economic growth, a clean environment, consumer safety, support for science and technology, and the like. But the effective recognition of citizens as equal adults with the capacity to make political choices is a minimal condition for being a liberal democracy.

Authoritarian governments, by contrast, fail to recognize the equal dignity of their citizens. They may pretend to do so through flowery constitutions such as those in China or Iran that list copious citizen rights, but where the reality is different. In relatively benevolent dictatorships, such as those of Lee Kuan Yew in Singapore or China under Deng Xiaoping, the state adopted a paternalistic attitude toward its citizens. Ordinary people were regarded as children who needed protection from a wise parent, the state; they could not be trusted to run their own affairs. In the worst dictatorships, such as those of Stalin and Hitler, large swaths of the population—kulaks (rich peasants), the bourgeoisie, Jews, the disabled, non-Aryans—were regarded as subhuman trash that could be discarded in the name of collective good.

The desire for the state to recognize one's basic dignity has been at the core of democratic movements since the French Revolution. A state guaranteeing equal political rights was the only rational way to resolve the contradictions that Hegel saw in the relationship between master and slave, where only the master was recognized. This is what drove Americans to protest during the civil rights movement, South Africans to stand up against apartheid, Mohamed Bouazizi to immolate himself, and other protesters to risk their lives in Yangon, Burma, or in the Maidan or Tahrir Square, or in countless other confrontations over the centuries.

6

EXPRESSIVE INDIVIDUALISM

The French Revolution unleashed what would become two different versions of identity politics across the world, though that term was not used to describe either phenomenon at the time. One stream demanded the recognition of the dignity of individuals, and the other the dignity of collectivities.

The first, individualistic stream began with the premise that all human beings were born free and were equal in their desire for freedom. Political institutions were created to preserve as much of that natural freedom as possible, consistent with the need for a common social life. Liberal democracies put the equal protection of individual autonomy at the core of their moral projects.

But what was meant by autonomy? Martin Luther, as we have seen, stood in a long Christian tradition that saw mankind's freedom as a gift from God that gave human beings dignity above the rest of the natural world.* But that freedom was

---

* Strictly speaking, Luther believed that faith was a gift from God, the result

limited to the ability to have faith and to follow God's law. Kant continued in this tradition, providing a secularized version of autonomy centered on the human ability to make moral choices based on abstract rules of reason. Human dignity for Kant was grounded in his view that all individuals were uncaused causes, capable of exercising genuine free will in a fashion not subject to the laws of physics. But Kant's rules such as the categorical imperative were not the objects of individual human choice; they were derived through philosophical reasoning and applied categorically to all human beings.

In this tradition, then, human dignity centers on an individual's ability to make proper moral choices, whether defined by religion or by secular reason.

The idea that dignity is rooted in human moral choice has received political recognition by becoming embedded in a significant number of modern democratic constitutions, including those of Germany, Italy, Ireland, Japan, Israel, and South Africa. For example, article I, section 1, of the German Basic Law of 1949 states, "The dignity of man is inviolable. To respect and protect it shall be the duty of all public authority." Similarly, section 10 of the South African constitution states, "Everyone has inherent dignity and the right to have their dignity respected and protected." The South African Constitutional Court has noted, "A right to dignity is an acknowledgment of the intrinsic worth of human beings."

None of these constitutions defines precisely what human

---

of God's grace, and was not something that could simply be willed by individuals. The Calvinists carried this doctrine further, believing that individuals were predestined either to be saved or not; they had no agency in the outcome. Nonetheless, under both doctrines faith was a characteristic of the inner self and still enjoined obedience to God's law, the content of which was not subject to human choice.

dignity is, and scarcely a politician in the Western world if pressed could explain its theoretical basis. To understand the provenance of such references to human dignity, one needs to look at the lexical origins of the words used, and the historical path by which they came to be written. The Kantian origin of the concept of dignity is evident in both the German and the South African cases. The German law's use of the word *inviolable* implies that all other rights are subordinated to this fundamental right and harks back to the categorical imperative, as does the South African reference to "intrinsic worth."[1] The Christian origins of the right to dignity are evidenced by the fact that it was Christian Democratic parties primarily that pushed for constitutional protections of dignity, beginning with the Irish constitution of 1937. None of these constitutions mentions Christianity explicitly, however, or seeks to link political rights to religious belief.[2]

The Anglo-American liberal tradition that began with Hobbes and Locke and continued through nineteenth-century thinkers such as John Stuart Mill took a less metaphysical approach to autonomy. This tradition does not build autonomy around free will; freedom is simply the ability to pursue one's desires and passions free of external constraint. (For Hobbes, human beings are like machines propelled forward by their desires; will is simply "the last appetite in deliberating," or an individual's strongest desire.) As a consequence, the word *dignity*, with its Christian-Kantian overtones, does not appear in the U.S. Constitution, or in founding documents such as the Federalist Papers.[3] Nonetheless, the Hobbesian notion that human beings are fundamentally equal in their natural freedom becomes the basis for the political rights on which the social contract is based. Hobbes's natural right to life becomes embedded in the American Declaration of Independence as part of the right to "life, liberty, and the pursuit of happiness." Thus a slightly different premise concerning the nature of autonomy leads to a similar regime dedicated to the equal protection of individual rights.

The liberal political tradition institutionalized one version of individual autonomy, by granting equal rights to citizens. But Rousseau's version of autonomy pointed to something deeper and richer than "mere" political participation. He saw within himself a "plenitude" of feeling that was suppressed by society; his was an unhappy consciousness that was deeply alienated by the society and struggled for liberation. As Charles Taylor explains:

> This is the powerful moral ideal that has come down to us. It accords crucial moral importance to a kind of contact with myself, with my own inner nature, which it sees as in danger of being lost, partly through the pressures towards outward conformity, but also because in taking an instrumental stance to myself, I may have lost the capacity to listen to this inner voice.[4]

This was part of the moral revaluation that began with Luther. The traditional Christian understanding of the inner self saw it as the site of original sin: we are full of evil desires that lead us to contravene God's law; external social rules, set by the Universal Church, lead us to suppress these desires. Rousseau followed Luther, but flipped the latter's valuation: the inner self is good or at least has the potential for being good; it is the surrounding moral rules that are bad. But for Rousseau, freedom is not just the moral choice to accept moral rules; it becomes the full expression of the feelings and emotions that constitute the authentic inner self. These feelings and emotions are often best expressed in art.

As Lionel Trilling brilliantly explained in his book *Sincerity and Authenticity*, European literature post-Rousseau saw the rise of a genre of writing that began with Diderot's *Rameau's Nephew* and Goethe's *Sufferings of Young Werther*, which celebrated the artist who is unable to find a home in society, who seeks the authentic expression of his or her creative genius. Figures such as Vincent van Gogh or Franz Kafka, unappreciated in their own time, became iconic symbols of the obtuseness of a philistine society that could not appreciate the depths of individuality they represented.

This shift in literary sensibilities mirrored a deeper and more fundamental breakdown of moral consensus in Europe. The institutional church, which had defined the region's moral horizon, came under increasing attack from Enlightenment figures such as Voltaire for its association with the predemocratic political status quo. But the underlying truth of Christianity was itself increasingly questioned, such as by the early nineteenth-century liberal theologian David Strauss, whose *Life of Jesus* suggested that the latter should be understood as a mere historical figure and not the literal Son of God.[5] This trend culminated by the late nineteenth century in the thought of Friedrich Nietzsche, who granted that the Christian God once lived, establishing a clear moral horizon for European society. But God had since died with the breakdown of belief, leaving a moral void that could be filled with alternative values. Unlike traditional moralists Nietzsche celebrated this fact because it enormously expanded the scope for human autonomy: human beings were free not just to accept the moral law, per Luther and Kant, but to create that law for themselves. In

Nietzsche's thought, the highest form of artistic expression was value creation itself. The most supremely autonomous person was his figure Zarathustra, who could declare the revaluation of all values in the wake of the death of the Christian God.

Modern liberal societies are heirs to the moral confusion left by the disappearance of a shared religious horizon. Their constitutions protect individual dignity and individual rights, and that dignity seems to be centered on individuals' ability to make moral choices. But what is the scope of those choices? Is choice limited to acceptance or rejection of a set of moral rules established by the surrounding society, or does true autonomy include the ability to make up those rules as well? With the decline during the twentieth century in Western societies of a shared belief in Christianity, different rules and values from other cultures began displacing traditional ones, as well as the option of not believing at all. Individual choice in areas outside of morals began to expand with the market economy and the general social mobility that it required: people could pick their occupations, marriage partners, domiciles, and brand of toothpaste. It seemed logical that they should have some choice in moral values as well. By the late twentieth century, the understanding of the scope of individual autonomy had broadened immensely in most modern democracies, leading to an efflorescence of what is sometimes termed expressive individualism. A clear line ran from Nietzsche's work *Beyond Good and Evil* to the assertion by U.S. Supreme Court justice Anthony Kennedy, in the 1992 decision *Planned Parenthood v. Casey*, that liberty is "the right to define one's own concept of existence, of meaning, of the universe, and of the mystery of human life."[6]

The problem with this understanding of autonomy is that shared values serve the important function of making social life possible. If we do not agree on a minimal common culture, we cannot cooperate on shared tasks and will not regard the same institutions as legitimate; indeed, we will not even be able to communicate with one another absent a common language with mutually understood meanings.

The other problem with this expansive understanding of individual autonomy is that not everyone is a Nietzschean superman seeking to revalue all values. Human beings are intensely social creatures whose emotional inclinations drive them to want to conform to the norms surrounding them. When a stable, shared moral horizon disappears and is replaced by a cacophony of competing value systems, the vast majority of people do not rejoice at their newfound freedom of choice. Rather, they feel an intense insecurity and alienation because they do not know who their true self is. This crisis of identity leads in the opposite direction from expressive individualism, to the search for a common identity that will rebind the individual to a social group and reestablish a clear moral horizon. This psychological fact lays the groundwork for nationalism.

Most people do not have infinite depths of individuality that is theirs alone. What they believe to be their true inner self is actually constituted by their relationships with other people, and by the norms and expectations that those others provide. A person living in Barcelona who suddenly realizes her real identity is Catalan rather than Spanish is simply excavating a lower layer of social identity that has been laid down beneath the one nearer to the surface.

The politics of recognition and dignity had reached a fork by the early nineteenth century. One fork led to the universal recognition of individual rights, and thence to liberal societies that sought to provide citizens with an ever-expanding scope of individual autonomy. The other fork led to assertions of collective identity, of which the two major manifestations were nationalism and politicized religion. Late-nineteenth-century Europe saw the rise both of liberal and democratic movements demanding universal individual recognition and the more ominous emergence of an exclusive nationalism that would eventually trigger the world wars of the early twentieth century. In the contemporary Muslim world, collective identity is taking the form of Islamism—that is, the demand for recognition of a special status for Islam as the basis of political community.

This twofold directionality—toward universal recognition of individual rights, and toward collective recognition based on nation—was evident in the writings of Jean-Jacques Rousseau, who at different moments celebrated both the peaceful solitary dreamer and the martial general will. The two were present from the early days of the French Revolution itself, which flew two banners: a universal one promoting the Rights of Man that was indifferent to national borders, and a national French one that sought to defend the French *patrie* from invasion by foreigners. When the Revolution was hijacked by Napoleon, he pursued both goals simultaneously, using military power to spread the liberal Code Napoléon while imposing French suzerainty over the parts of Europe he conquered.

This dual character was present as well both in the Arab Spring and in Ukraine's Revolution of Dignity. Millions of Arab citizens throughout the Middle East could sympathize with Mohamed Bouazizi, but not all of them wanted to live in a society that recognized the equal rights of all citizens, regardless of religion. Authoritarian regimes such as those of Zine al-Abidine Ben Ali in Tunisia and Hosni Mubarak in Egypt were equal-opportunity dictators, secularists suppressing not just Western-oriented liberals but Islamists as well. The advocates of a liberal successor regime contended with Islamists who sought a religious definition of national identity. When the Islamist Muslim Brotherhood took power in Egypt through democratic elections in 2012, they threatened to create a dictatorship of their own, leading the military to stage a coup in June 2013. Many former Egyptian liberals supported this takeover to prevent Egypt from becoming an Islamist republic.

Similarly, the Maidan Revolution of Dignity was based on a coalition of Western-oriented liberals who wanted Ukraine to join the European Union and become a normal European country. But they joined hands with Ukrainian nationalists from groups such as Right Sector, who sought to protect a separate Ukrainian cultural identity and were less interested in a liberal, open Ukraine.

We will return to the question of how individualist understandings of dignity and autonomy evolved in liberal societies over the past century in chapters 10 and 11. In the meantime, we will look more closely at two forms of collective identity, those based on nationalism and on religion.

Both nationalism and Islamism—that is, political Islam—can be seen as two sides of the same coin. Both are expressions of a hidden or suppressed group identity that seeks public recognition. And both phenomena arise in similar circumstances, when economic modernization and rapid social change undermine older forms of community and replace them with a confusing pluralism of alternative forms of association.

7

NATIONALISM AND RELIGION

Luther, Rousseau, Kant, and Hegel understood dignity in different ways. But they were universalists insofar as they believed in the equality of dignity of all human beings based on their potential for inner freedom. Yet the demand for recognition often takes a more particular form, centering on the dignity of a particular group that has been marginalized or disrespected. For many, the inner self that needed to be made visible was not that of a generic human being, but of a particular kind of person from a particular place and observing particular customs. These partial identities could be based on nation, or they could be based on religion. Because they demanded recognition of the dignity of the group in question, they turned into political movements that we label nationalism or Islamism.

The thinker who was critical in shifting the focus of recognition struggles away from an individual if universally shared freedom to collective freedom based on particular national or cultural characteristics was Johann Gottfried von Herder, a late-eighteenth-century student and contemporary of Kant. Herder has often been attacked as the father of modern European ethno-nationalism, a writer who celebrated the primitive *Volk*, or people, and was a distant precursor of Adolf Hitler.

This view is highly unfair to a thinker who has been inadequately read and studied in the English-speaking world. Herder shared many of Kant's Enlightenment views about human equality, but spent far more time reading broadly the travel literature of Europeans who had visited obscure foreign lands and recorded their observations of local customs. In *Reflections on the Philosophy of the History of Mankind*, Herder states clearly that there is a single human species, and he attacks other authors who have tried to establish hierarchies among the world's races. He empathizes with the pain of Africans taken in slavery and asserts that cultures can be measured by their treatment of women. In a period well before the discovery of modern genetics, he had an amazingly sophisticated understanding of the complex interaction between biological characteristics and environment in shaping behavior.[1]

Nonetheless, Herder argued that each human community is unique and separate from its neighbors. He notes that climate and geography have had huge impacts on the customs of different peoples, each of which expresses its own "genius" in the ways they have adapted to local circumstances. Unlike Hegel, who simply wrote off Africa as irrelevant to human history, Herder took a sympathetic view of non-European cultures. Like a contemporary cultural anthropologist, he was more interested in describing than in evaluating other peoples. And, in an age well before the big European push to colonize the globe, he issued a warning that contemporary nation-builders might take to heart: "Let it not be imagined, that human art can with despotic power convert at once a foreign region into another Europe."[2]

Herder's link to modern nationalism is clear. His work sought to promote an appreciation for the unique customs and traditions of each of the world's people. Like Rousseau, he did not believe that those who lived in later historical times were necessarily better or happier than the "primitive" peoples who came before. He agreed that society could force us to play false roles. In doing so, he staked out a position very different from that of Hegel, who in the following generation would argue that history was universal and progressive.[3]

Herder applied his idea of cultural authenticity to the Germany of his time, which was divided into countless petty principalities, many of which sought to emulate the splendor and culture of the French court at Versailles. Herder argued that the Germans needed to take pride in their own culture and traditions rather than seeking to be second-rate Frenchmen. He sought recognition, not for an abstraction like the "Man" in the Rights of Man, but rather for his particular people and, by extension, every other human community.

The "long nineteenth century" that stretched from the French Revolution to the outbreak of World War I in 1914 saw two versions of dignity and two approaches to identity in competition with each other. The first sought recognition of the universal Rights of Man (not, at that point, necessarily of women as well). The other sought recognition of the dignity of particular peoples who had been oppressed or held in bondage by others. These different versions of dignity, universal and national, contended with each other over decades; the revolutions of 1848, for example, were fought in the name both of liberal rights and of national self-assertion. By the early twentieth century, the liberal version of dignity was joined by another universalist doctrine, Marxist socialism, which would fight for the rights of proletarians. Both the liberal and the socialist movements contended with nationalism through the two world wars; after fascism's defeat in 1945, the two universal doctrines emerged as the poles around which global politics was organized during the Cold War. But nationalism was never fully discredited, despite institutions such as the European Union that were designed to keep it in check, and has reemerged as a new force in the twenty-first century.

Ideas were important to understanding the rise of nationalism, but important economic and social changes were also taking place that prepared the ground for its emergence in nineteenth-century Europe. The old European order of the Middle Ages was hierarchical and stratified according to social class; feudalism divided Europe's populations into countless tiny jurisdictions and was designed to lock them into place.

A modern market economy, by contrast, depends on the free movement of labor, capital, and ideas from places where they are abundant to places where they can earn a high return. The universal recognition offered by liberal societies was particularly conducive to capitalist development, since it protected individuals' freedom to engage in commerce from the state and preserved their right to own private property. It is therefore not surprising that liberalism became the handmaiden of economic growth, and that two of the most liberal societies of the time, Britain and the United States, were leading drivers of industrialization during the nineteenth and early twentieth centuries.

But a modern market economy required something like nationalism and identity based on nation as well. Nationalism is a doctrine that political borders ought to correspond to cultural communities, with culture defined largely by shared language.

In premodern Europe, France was a mosaic of different tongues such as Breton, Picard, Flemish, and Provençal, in addition to Parisian French. Elsewhere in Europe, peasants often spoke a different language from their lords in the local manor; Latin was the court language of the Habsburg Empire until the nineteenth century. Throughout Central and Eastern Europe, Germans were mixed with Poles, Moravians, Ukrainians, Hungarians, and many others in small, self-regarding communities. All of this inhibited the mobility required by labor markets in an industrializing society. As the social anthropologist Ernest Gellner explained, "A society has emerged based on a high-powered technology and the expectancy of sustained growth, which requires both a mobile division of labour, and sustained, frequent and precise communication between strangers." This necessitates a uniform national language, and a state-sponsored educational system to promote national culture. "The employability, dignity, security and self-respect of individuals . . . now hinges on their *education* . . . Modern man is not loyal to a monarch or a land or faith, whatever he may say, but to a culture."[4]

But nationalism was also born out of the acute anxieties bred by industrialization. Consider the situation of a young peasant, Hans, who grows up in a small village in Saxony. Hans's life in the little village is fixed: he is living in the same house as his parents and grandparents; he is engaged to a girl whom his parents found acceptable; he was baptized by the local priest; and he plans to continue working the same plot of land as his father. It doesn't occur to Hans to ask "Who am I?" since that question has already been answered for him by the people around him. However, he hears that big opportunities are opening up in the rapidly industrializing Ruhr valley, so he travels to Düsseldorf to get a job in a steel factory there.

Hans is now living in a dormitory with hundreds of other young men like himself, coming from all over northwestern Germany. People speak in different dialects; some of the people he meets are not German at all, but Dutch or French. He is no longer under the thumb of his parents and local priest and finds people with different religious affiliations than those in his village. He is still committed to marrying his fiancée but tempted by some of the local women he has met, and he feels a bracing sense of freedom in his personal life.

At the same time Hans is troubled. Back in his village, he was surrounded by friends and relatives, who knew him and would support him in times of sickness or a bad harvest. He does not have that kind of certainty about the new friends and acquaintances he has made and is not sure that his new employer, a big corporation, will look after his interests. He is told that some Communist agitators are pushing to create a trade union in his factory, but he has heard bad things about them and doesn't trust them either. The newspapers are full of conflicting stories about fights in the parliament, and he is not sure whom to believe. Hans suspects that all of these quarreling political parties are selfish and not interested in representing him. His part of Germany has become part of an enormous *Reich* of which he can feel proud, but one that is barreling forward to an uncertain future. He feels lonely and disconnected from his surroundings; he feels nostalgia for his village, but doesn't want to return there, as that would be a sign of personal defeat. For the first time in his life, Hans can make choices about how to live his life, but he wonders who he really is and what he would like to be. The question of identity, which would never have been a problem back in his village, now becomes central.

Hans's personal story was characterized by the nineteenth-century social theorist Ferdinand Tönnies as the shift from

Gemeinschaft to *Gesellschaft,* or from (village) community to (urban) society. It was experienced by millions of Europeans during the nineteenth century and is now happening in rapidly industrializing societies such as China and Vietnam.

The psychological dislocation engendered by the transition from *Gemeinschaft* to *Gesellschaft* laid the basis for an ideology of nationalism based on an intense nostalgia for an imagined past of strong community in which the divisions and confusions of a pluralist modern society did not exist. Well before the rise of Adolf Hitler in the 1930s, German writers were lamenting the loss of *Gemeinschaft* and what they saw as the perversions of a cosmopolitan liberal society.

The historian Fritz Stern analyzed a number of these early ideologists of German identity, such as the hugely influential polemicist and biblical scholar Paul de Lagarde. Lagarde lived in Bismarck's newly unified Germany of the late nineteenth century, when the country was experiencing an economic miracle of growth, industrialization, and burgeoning military and political power. Yet Lagarde, in countless articles and pamphlets (collected as his *German Writings* in 1886), saw around him nothing but cultural decay: the German spirit had declined into self-seeking as a result of liberal doctrines based on rationality and science. The old Germany was one of virtues and strong community that needed to be brought back. He imagined a new religion that would fuse Christianity with the "national characteristics of the Germans," a faith that would become the basis for a new national identity. Lagarde wrote, "Once a nation, [a people] has but one will, and all conflict is banished." Something of an academic outcast, he had never achieved the fame he thought he deserved for his interpretive work on the Septuagint; unity with the German people was at once a solution to his personal loneliness and a source of the dignity he could not achieve as an individual scholar.[5]

Lagarde, like Julius Langbehn, Arthur Moeller van den Bruck, and other nineteenth-century German nationalists, saw the German people as victims of outside forces. Lagarde had a conspiratorial view of why German culture had decayed: the Jews were the bearers of liberal modernity, inserting themselves into the cultural life of the new modern Germany, bringing with them universalist ideas of democracy and socialism that undermined the unity of the German people. To reestablish German greatness, the Jews would have to be banished from the new order he envisioned.

Intellectuals from Friedrich Nietzsche to Ernst Troeltsch to Thomas Mann read Lagarde sympathetically, and his works would be widely distributed by the Nazis.[6] He spoke to the anxieties of people making the transition from agrarian village society to modern, urban industrial life, a transition that for millions of Europeans experiencing it pushed the question of identity to the forefront. This was the moment in which the personal became the political. The answer given to a confused peasant like Hans from ideologists such as Lagarde was simple: You are a proud German, heir to an ancient culture, connected by your common language to all of the millions of other Germans scattered across Central and Eastern Europe. The lonely and confused worker now had a clear sense of dignity, a dignity that, he now realized, was disrespected by bad people who had somehow infiltrated his society.

The new form of identity based on shared culture and language unleashed new passions, since these new cultural groups lived in old jurisdictions such as the Austro-Hungarian Empire that were based on dynastic ties rather than culture. Uniting scattered Germans under a single *Reich* would become a political project over the next three generations undertaken by leaders from Bismarck to Hitler. Other nationalities—Serbs, Poles, Hungarians, Russians—were also seeking to create or consolidate states based on ethno-nationalism, which would lead Europe into two devastating world wars in the early twentieth century.

Identity also became a critical issue in the then-colonial world. The parts of Asia, Africa, and Latin America dominated by the European powers were not as a whole industrializing as Europe was. They were instead going through what has sometimes been labeled modernization without development— that is, urbanization and rapid social change without sustained economic growth. They acquired new capital cities with a small indigenous elite that collaborated with the colonial powers in administering their territories. Members of this elite received European educations and spoke the metropolitan language. But they felt an intense inner conflict between these acquired identities and the indigenous traditions with which they had grown up. As nationalism spread in Europe, it took root as well in Europe's colonies, leading by the middle of the twentieth century to open revolts in such places as India, Vietnam, Kenya, and Algeria in the name of national liberation. Nationalism in the colonial world led to efforts by intellectuals to revolutionize culture as well. Black writers such as Aimé Césaire, Léon Damas, and Léopold Senghor, for example, developed the concept of Négritude to help blacks take pride in their race and heritage, reversing the colonial regimes' denigration of them.

Ernest Gellner was a major theorist of nationalism, and he suggested that modern Islamism needed to be seen through a similar lens of modernization and identity. Both nationalism and Islamism are rooted in modernization. The shift from

Gemeinschaft to *Gesellschaft* has been occurring in the contemporary Middle East, as peasants or bedouin have left the countryside for cities such as Cairo, Amman, and Algiers. Alternatively, millions of Muslims experienced modernization by migrating to Europe or other Western countries in search of better lives, settling in Marseille or Rotterdam or Bradford and confronting there an alien culture. In other cases, the modern world came to them in their villages via satellite TV from stations such as Al Jazeera or CNN International. People living in traditional villages with limited choices are suddenly confronted with a pluralistic world with very different ways of life in which their traditional norms are not respected.

The identity problem is particularly acute for young second-generation Muslims growing up in immigrant communities in Western Europe. They are living in largely secular societies with Christian roots that do not provide public support for their religious values or practices. Their parents often came from closed village communities offering localized versions of Islam, such as Sufi saint worship. Like many children of immigrants, they are eager to distance themselves from their families' old-fashioned ways of life. But they are not easily integrated into their new European surroundings: rates of youth unemployment, particularly for Muslims, are upward of 30 percent, and in many European countries a link is still perceived between ethnicity and membership in the dominant cultural community—an issue that we will return to in later chapters.

Under these circumstances, confusion about identity becomes acute, just as it was for newly urbanized Europeans in the nineteenth century. For some Muslims today, the answer to this confusion has not been membership in a nation, but membership in a larger religious group—an *umma*, or community of believers, represented by a political party such as Egypt's Muslim Brotherhood or Turkey's Justice and Development Party or Tunisia's Ennahda. Like classic nationalists, contemporary Islamists have both a diagnosis of the problem and a clear solution: you are part of a proud and ancient community; the outside world doesn't respect you as a Muslim; we offer you a way to connect to your true brothers and sisters, where you will be a member of a great community of believers that stretches across the world.

This assertion of pride in one's identity may explain the cultural shifts that have been taking place across the Muslim world over the past generation. After a prolonged period in which it was fashionable for educated people from the Middle East to adopt Western customs and garb, a large number of young Muslim women in Egypt, Turkey, Jordan, and other Middle Eastern countries have started to wear the hijab or headscarf; some have taken to even more restrictive forms of female dress such as the full-face veil, or niqab. Many of these women are indeed pious Muslims, but others are not particularly religious; wearing the hijab is rather a signal of identity, a marker that they are proud of their culture and not afraid to be publicly identified as a Muslim.

Mainstream Islamist parties such as those mentioned above have been willing to participate in democratic politics and have won victories at the polls that have led them into government. Despite their public avowals of commitment to democracy, their secular opponents often remain highly suspicious of their long-term agenda. The same could be said about nationalists, either in the nineteenth century or today: they often play by democratic rules, but harbor potentially illiberal tendencies due to their longings for unity and community.

As was the case with nationalism, more extreme versions of politicized religion have been proffered by ideologists such as

Osama bin Laden or Abu Bakr al-Baghdadi, the founder of the Islamic State. Their narrative is far more focused on victimization by the United States, Israel, the Assad regime in Syria, or Iran, and they advocate an even tighter community bound by a shared commitment to violence and direct political action.

The French Middle Eastern scholar Olivier Roy has pointed out that many recent terrorists, such as those who staged the Bataclan attacks in Paris in 2015, have a similar background: they are second-generation European Muslims who have rejected the Islam of their parents. (About 25 percent of the new generation of jihadis are converts to Islam with personal stories similar to those of jihadis who were born Muslim.)[7] In their early years they appeared to be westernized, drinking alcohol and smoking weed, dating girls, watching sports, and otherwise seeming to fit into their surroundings. Yet many failed to find regular jobs and began a descent into petty crime and run-ins with the police. They lived at the margins of their own communities, with no history of great piety or interest in religion, until they are suddenly "born-again" by watching videos of radical imams or being converted by a prison preacher. When they showed up in Syria with a long beard and toting an AK-47 or staged a murderous attack on their fellow Europeans, their families always professed surprise and incomprehension at the transformation. Roy has described this not as the radicalization of Islam, but the Islamicization of radicalism—that is, a process that draws from the same alienation that drove earlier generations of extremists, whether nationalists such as Paul de Lagarde or Communists such as Leon Trotsky.[8]

Roy's profile suggests that the motives behind jihadist terrorism are more personal and psychological than religious and reflects the acute problem of identity that certain individuals face. Second-generation European Muslims in particular are caught between two cultures, that of their parents, which they reject, and that of their adopted country, which doesn't fully accept them. Radical Islam by contrast offers them community, acceptance, and dignity. Roy argues that the number of Muslims who become terrorists or suicide bombers is minuscule compared to the total global population of over a billion Muslims. Poverty and deprivation, or simple anger over American foreign policy, does not inevitably lead people to extremism. Many terrorists have come from comfortable middle-class backgrounds, and many were apolitical and unconcerned with global politics for most of their lives. Neither these issues nor any kind of genuine religiosity drove them so much as the need for a clear identity, meaning, and a sense of pride. They realized that they had an inner, unrecognized self that the outside world was trying to suppress.[9]

Olivier Roy has been sharply criticized for his interpretation of contemporary jihadism and his downplaying of its religious dimension, particularly by his fellow French scholar of Islam Gilles Kepel. Kepel argues that the turn toward violence and extremism cannot be understood apart from the religious doctrines being promoted around the world, and in particular the brand of ultraconservative Salafism exported out of Saudi Arabia. He accuses Roy and much of the French left for exonerating Islam by pretending that the problem of jihadism has little to do with a particular religion. Others have pointed out that many terrorists do not fit the description offered by Roy.[10]

The Roy-Kepel debate centers around a critical question: Is the rise of Islamist radicalism in the early twenty-first century best understood as an identity problem, or is it at base a genuinely religious phenomenon? That is, is it the by-product of the sociology of our age and the dislocations brought on by modernization and globalization, or does it represent a timeless feature of one particular religion, and the independent role of ideas in motivating human behavior? Answering this question is critical to knowing how to deal with the problem in practical terms.

These alternative interpretations are not, however, mutually exclusive; they may complement one another. Olivier Roy is correct in noting that the huge majority of the world's Muslims are not radicals, which implies that explanations for extremism must be rooted in individual stories and social settings. Yet Kepel is correct that disaffected young European Muslims are not becoming anarcho-syndicalists or Communists, but jihadis preaching a particular version of Islam. Moreover, earlier generations of radicalized youth did not seek to blow themselves up in suicide attacks; specific ideas motivate this fashion.

Social change and ideology were also separate drivers of European nationalism. The identity confusion created by rapid modernization laid the groundwork for nationalism in Germany and other European countries. But it cannot be solely blamed for the rise of the particularly virulent and extreme version of nationalism represented by Adolf Hitler and his National Socialist Party. Other countries such as France, Britain, and the United States underwent similar social changes; they may have been tempted but ultimately did not succumb to similar radical nationalist doctrines. It took a brilliant political entrepreneur and ideologue such as Hitler, and the huge economic dislocations experienced by Germany in the 1920s and '30s, to permit the rise of the Nazi movement.

Similarly, in the Middle East today, many Muslims feel identity confusion and have turned to religion as an answer to "Who am I?" This turn may take the innocuous form of wearing a hijab to work or a burkini at the beach. But for some it takes a more violent and dangerous turn in the form of political activism and terrorism. The extremist forms of Muslim identity being proffered in the early twenty-first century are no more compatible with international peace than were the nationalist doctrines of the early twentieth century.

Both nationalism and Islamism can thus be seen as a species of identity politics. Stating this does not do justice to the full complexity or specificity of either phenomenon. But they nonetheless have a number of important similarities. They both appeared on the world stage at moments of social transition from traditional isolated agrarian societies to modern ones connected to a broader and more diverse world. They both provide an ideology that explains why people feel lonely and confused, and both peddle in victimhood that lays the blame for an individual's unhappy situation on groups of outsiders. And they both demand recognition of dignity in restrictive ways: not for all human beings, but for members of a particular national or religious group.

8

THE WRONG ADDRESS

One of the striking characteristics of global politics in the second decade of the twenty-first century is that the dynamic new forces shaping it are nationalist or religious parties and politicians, the two faces of identity politics, rather than the class-based left-wing parties that were so prominent in the politics of the twentieth century.

Nationalism may have been sparked initially by industrialization and modernization, but it has in no way disappeared from the world, including in those countries that have been industrially developed for generations. A host of new populist nationalist leaders claiming democratic legitimacy via elections have emphasized national sovereignty and national traditions in the interest of "the people." These leaders include Russia's Putin, Turkey's Erdoğan, Hungary's Orbán, Poland's Kaczynski, and finally Donald J. Trump in the United States, whose campaign slogans were Make America Great Again and America First. The Brexit movement in the United Kingdom has not had a clear leader, yet here too the basic impulse was a reassertion of national sovereignty. Populist parties are waiting in the wings in France, the Netherlands, and all over Scandinavia. Nationalist rhetoric has not been limited to these leaders, however; Prime Ministers Narendra Modi of India and Shinzo Abe of Japan have both been identified with nationalist causes, as has Xi Jinping of China, who has emphasized a socialism with distinctively Chinese characteristics.

At the same time, religion has been on the upswing as a political phenomenon. This is most obviously true in the Arab Middle East, where the 2011 Arab Spring was derailed by Islamist groups such as the Muslim Brotherhood and more radical terrorist organizations such as the Islamic State. While the latter has been nearly defeated militarily in Syria and Iraq, Islamist movements continue to spread in countries such as Bangladesh, Thailand, and the Philippines. In Indonesia, the popular Christian governor of Jakarta, Basuki Tjahaja Purnama (Ahok), was attacked for alleged blasphemy by increasingly self-confident Islamist groups and eventually jailed after narrowly losing his reelection bid. Islam is not the only form of politicized religion, however. Prime Minister Modi's Bharatiya Janata Party (BJP) is explicitly based on a Hindu understanding of Indian national identity. A militant form of political Buddhism has been spreading in South and Southeast Asian countries such as Sri Lanka and Myanmar, where it has clashed with Muslim and Hindu groups. And religious groups form part of the conservative coalition in democracies such as Japan, Poland, and the United States. In Israel, a political order that had been dominated for more than a generation after independence by two European-style ideological parties, Labor and Likud, has seen an ever greater proportion of votes going to religious parties such as Shas or Agudath Israel.

The old class-based left has, by contrast, been in long-term decline around the globe. Communism collapsed in 1989–91, though versions of it hang on in North Korea and Cuba. Social democracy, one of the dominant forces shaping Western European politics in the two generations following World War II, has been in retreat. The German Social Democrats, who received over 40 percent of the vote in 1998, fell to just over 20 percent by 2016, while the French Socialist Party all but disappeared in 2017. Overall, center-left parties declined from 30 to 24 percent of the vote between 1993 and 2017 in Northern Europe, 36 to 21 percent in Southern Europe, and 25 to 18 percent in Central Europe. They are still major players, but a trend is clear.[1]

Left-wing parties throughout Europe shifted to the center in the 1990s, accepting the logic of the market economy, and many became hard to distinguish from their coalition partners on the center-right. There were always Communist and other leftist groups in the Middle East during the Cold War; a self-styled Communist regime even came to power in South Yemen. Since then, however, they have been totally marginalized and left behind by Islamist parties. Left-wing populism made a strong showing primarily in parts of Latin America in the 1990s and 2000s, with the rise of Hugo Chávez in Venezuela, Luiz Inácio Lula da Silva in Brazil, and the Kirchners in Argentina. But this wave has already retreated, with the self-immolation of Venezuela under Chavez's successor, Nicolás Maduro. The strong showings of Jeremy Corbyn in the United Kingdom and Bernie Sanders in the United States may be harbingers of a recovery, but parties of the left are nowhere the dominant forces they were through the late twentieth century.

The global weakness of the left is in many ways a surprising outcome, given the rise of global inequality over the past three decades. By global inequality, I am referring to the rise of inequality within individual countries, rather than between countries. The gap between rich and poor countries has closed as high levels of growth have occurred not just in East Asia but in Latin America and sub-Saharan Africa. But as the economist Thomas Piketty has shown, within-country inequality around the world has seen a large increase since 1980; contrary to the long-accepted theory of the economist Simon Kuznets, rich-country incomes have been diverging rather than converging.[2] Hardly a single region of the world has not seen the rise of a new class of oligarchs—billionaires who use their wealth politically to protect their family interests.[3]

The economist Branko Milanovic has devised a widely cited "elephant graph," which shows the relative gains in per capita income for different segments of the global income distribution. The world grew much richer through productivity gains and globalization from 1988 to 2008, but these gains were not equally distributed. Those in the twentieth to the seventieth percentiles had substantial increases in income, with even larger ones for those in the ninety-fifth percentile. But the part of the global population around the eightieth percentile experienced either stagnation or else marginal gains. This group largely corresponds to the working class in developed countries—that is, people with a high school education or less. While they remain much better off than those below them, they have lost significant ground to people in the top 10 percent of the distribution. Their relative status, in other words, fell sharply.

Within the developed world, inequality has been the most pronounced in Britain and the United States, the two countries that led the "neoliberal," pro–free market revolution of the 1980s under Margaret Thatcher and Ronald Reagan. In the United States, the strong economic growth of the 1980s and

TABLE 1

Relative Gain in Real Per Capita Income by Global Income Level, 1988–2008[4]

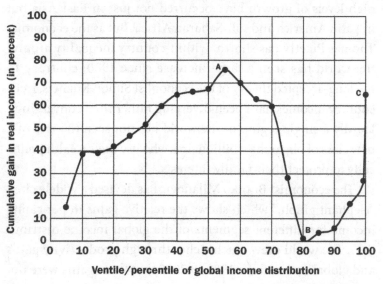

’90s was not evenly distributed, but went overwhelmingly to those with good educations. The old American working class, which thought of itself as the core of the middle class, steadily lost ground. According to a study by the International Monetary Fund, in a hollowing out of the middle class, individuals earning from 50 to 150 percent of median income fell from 58 to 47 percent of the population from 2000 to 2014. Only one-quarter of 1 percent did this by moving up into higher income brackets; an astonishing 3.25 percent moved down the income ladder.[5] This inequality was intensified by the financial crisis of 2008, in which the machinations and policy choices of the financial sector created an asset bubble whose bursting destroyed jobs and savings for millions of ordinary Americans, as well as countless others around the world.

Under these circumstances, one would expect to see a huge revival of a populist left in those countries experiencing the highest levels of inequality. Since the French Revolution, the left has defined itself as the party of economic equality, willing to use state power to redistribute wealth from rich to poor. Yet the aftermath of the global financial crisis has seen something of the opposite, a rise of right-wing populist nationalist forces across many parts of the developed world. This was nowhere more true than in the United States and Britain, where deindustrialization had ravaged the old working class. In the former, the financial crisis spawned the left-wing Occupy Wall Street movement and the right-wing Tea Party. The former marched and demonstrated, then fizzled out, while the latter succeeded in taking over both the Republican Party and much of Congress. In 2016, voters failed to endorse the most left-wing populist candidates, choosing nationalist politicians instead.

How do we explain the failure of the left to capitalize on rising global inequality, and the rise of the nationalist right in its place? This is not a new phenomenon: parties of the left have been losing out to nationalists for well over a hundred years, precisely among those poor or working-class constituencies that should have been their most solid base of support. The European working class lined up not under the banner of the Socialist International in 1914, but with their national governments as World War I began. This failure has befuddled Marxists for years; in the words of Ernest Gellner, they told themselves that

just as extreme Shi'ite Muslims hold that Archangel Gabriel made a mistake, delivering the Message to Mohamed when it was intended for Ali, so Marxists basically like to think that the spirit of history or human consciousness made a terrible boob. The awakening message was intended for *classes*, but by some terrible postal error was delivered to *nations*.[6]

Similarly, in the contemporary Middle East, a letter addressed to classes has been delivered instead to religions.

This postal delivery error occurred because of the way in which economic motivations are intertwined with identity issues in human behavior. To be poor is to be invisible to your fellow human beings, and the indignity of invisibility is often worse than the lack of resources.

9

INVISIBLE MAN

Economists assume that human beings are motivated by what they label "preferences" or "utilities," desires for material resources or goods. But they forget about thymos, the part of the soul that desires recognition by others, either as isothymia, recognition as equal in dignity to others, or megalothymia, recognition as superior. A great deal of what we conventionally take to be economic motivation driven by material needs or desires is in fact a thymotic desire for recognition of one's dignity or status.

Take the issue of equal pay for equal work, something that has been at the core of the women's rights movement for decades. While women have made huge gains over the past fifty years in the labor force, considerable attention has been paid to the glass ceilings that have kept women out of senior management positions or, more recently, from the upper ranks of tech firms in Silicon Valley. Much of the agenda of modern feminism has been set not by working-class women hoping to get jobs as firefighters or Marine grunts, but by educated professional women seeking to rise closer to the top of the social hierarchy.

Among this group, what is the real motive driving demands for equal pay? It is not economic in any conventional sense. A female lawyer who is passed over for partner or is made vice president but at a salary 10 percent lower than that of her male counterparts is in no sense economically deprived: she is likely to be in the very top of the national income distribution and faces little economic deprivation. If she and her male counterpart were paid twice their relative salaries, the problem would still remain.

Rather, the anger felt in such situations is not so much about resources as about justice: the pay she is awarded by the firm is important not so much because it provides needed resources, but rather because salary is a marker of dignity, and the firm is telling her that she is worth less than a man even though her qualifications and contributions are equal or even superior. Salary is a matter of *recognition*. She would feel equally aggrieved if she was given the same pay, but told that she would never hold a coveted title simply because she is a woman.

The connection between economic interest and recognition was well understood by the founder of modern political economy, Adam Smith, in his book *The Theory of Moral Sentiments*. Even in late-eighteenth-century Britain, he observed that the poor had basic necessities and did not suffer from gross material deprivation. They sought wealth for a different reason:

> To be observed, to be attended to, to be taken notice of with sympathy, complacency, and approbation, are all the advantages which we can propose to derive from it. It is the vanity, not the ease or the pleasure, which interests us. But

vanity is always founded upon the belief of our being the object of attention and approbation.

The rich man glories in his riches, because he feels that they naturally draw upon him the attention of the world, and that mankind are disposed to go along with him in all the agreeable emotions with which the advantages of his situation so readily inspire him . . . The poor man, on the contrary, is ashamed of his poverty. He feels that it either places him out of sight of mankind, or, that if they take any notice of him, they have, however, scarce any fellow-feeling with the misery and distress which he suffers.[1]

The rich man "glories in his riches." If one thinks about the class of global billionaires and asks what gets them out of bed every morning, the answer cannot be that they feel the lack of some necessity but cannot have it if they do not make another $100 million in the coming months. One can only have so many houses, boats, and airplanes before one loses count. Rather, they want other things: to have the biggest collection of Francis Bacon paintings, or to skipper the winning America's Cup yacht, or to build the largest charitable foundation. What they seek is not some absolute level of wealth, but rather status relative to that of other billionaires.

Something similar can be said of poverty in a wealthy country such as the United States, Germany, or Sweden. As conservatives never tire of pointing out, people living below the poverty line in the United States enjoy a remarkable level of material wealth, far higher than that of a poor person in sub-Saharan Africa: they own televisions, automobiles, and Air Jordans; they tend to suffer not from malnutrition but from obesity because they eat too much junk food.

There is of course material deprivation in the United States, in the lack of access to good education or health care. But the pain of poverty is felt more often as a loss of dignity: as Smith notes, the poor man's situation "places him out of sight of mankind," such that they have no fellow feeling for him. This was the basic insight of Ralph Ellison's classic novel, *Invisible Man*, about a black man moving from the American South to Harlem. The real indignity of racism in the North was that African-Americans were invisible to their white peers, not necessarily mistreated but simply not seen as fellow human beings. Consider that the next time you give money to a homeless person, but fail to make eye contact with him or her: you are relieving the material want, but failing to acknowledge the shared humanity between the beggar and you.

The connection of income to dignity also suggests why something like a universal guaranteed income as a solution to job loss from automation won't buy social peace or make people happy. Having a job conveys not just resources, but recognition by the rest of society that one is doing something socially valuable. Someone paid for doing nothing has no basis for pride.

The economist Robert Frank notes the connection between wealth and status and points out that the latter is often desired not for its absolute but for its relative value. He calls this a "positional good": I want that Tesla not because I care so much about global warming, but because it is trendy and expensive, and my neighbor is still driving a BMW. Human happiness is oftentimes more strongly connected to our relative than to our absolute status. Frank points out that in surveys, people with higher incomes report higher degrees of happiness. One might think this is related to absolute levels of income, except that people with comparable *relative* status report comparable levels of happiness regardless of their absolute wealth: upper-income Nigerians are just as happy as their German counterparts, despite the economic gap separating them. One compares oneself not globally to some absolute standard of wealth, but relative to a local group that one deals with socially.[2]

A great deal of evidence coming out of the natural sciences suggests that the desire for status—megalothymia—is rooted in human biology. Primates that achieve dominance or alpha male status within their local hierarchies have been widely observed as having higher levels of the neurotransmitter serotonin. Serotonin is associated with feelings of well-being and elation in human beings; that is why selective serotonin reuptake inhibitors such as Prozac and Zoloft are widely used in treating depression and low self-esteem.[3]

A further psychological fact suggests that certain things in contemporary politics are related more to status than to resources. One of the clear findings from experimental behavioral economics is that people are much more sensitive to losses than to gains. That is, they are likely to spend much more effort to avoid the loss of $100 than to receive an extra $100 in income.[4] This may explain a historical phenomenon noted by Samuel Huntington, namely that the most politically destabilizing group tends not to be the desperate poor, but rather middle classes who feel they are losing their status with respect to other groups. He cites Alexis de Tocqueville, who noted that the French Revolution was not triggered by indigent peasants, but by a rising middle class that suddenly saw its economic and political prospects sink in the decade before the Revolution. The poor tend to be politically disorganized and preoccupied with day-to-day survival. People who think of themselves as middle class, by contrast, have more time for political activity and are better educated and easier to mobilize. More important, they feel that their economic status entitles them to respect: they work hard at jobs that are useful to society, they raise families, and they carry out their responsibilities to society such as paying taxes. They know that they are not at the top of the economic heap, but they also have pride in not being indigent or dependent on government help to survive.* Middle-class people do not feel themselves to be at the margins of society; rather, they typically feel that they constitute the core of national identity.

Loss of middle-class status may explain one of the most bitter polarizations in contemporary politics, which has emerged in Thailand. The country has been riven by an intense polarization between "yellow shirts" and "red shirts," the former upper-class supporters of the monarchy and military and the latter supporters of the Thai Rak Thai party, led by Thaksin Shinawatra. This conflict, which closed down much of Bangkok in 2010 and resulted in a yellow-shirt-supported military coup, has alternatively been seen as a fight over ideology based on the redistribution programs that Thaksin and his sister Yingluck, prime minister from 2011 to 2014, provided to rural Thais, or else a fight about corruption. Federico Ferrara argues, however, that it is better seen as a fight over recognition. Traditional Thai society had been rigidly stratified based on perceived "Thai-ness," the geographical and ethnolinguistic distance of people from the elite in Bangkok. Decades of economic growth had raised up many of Thaksin's voters, who began to assert their provincial identities in ways that enraged the Bangkok elite.

---

* In the United States there is a great deal of confusion over the term *middle class*, since a large majority of Americans like to categorize themselves as middle class, even when they are well-to-do elites or people who in Europe would be characterized as working-class or even poor. The most politically relevant group would be those in the third or fourth quintiles of the national income distribution, who are the most vulnerable to stagnation or downward mobility.

It was often middle-class Thais who became the most politically engaged, and that explains why an apparently economic conflict became a zero-sum game driven by thymos.[5]

The perceived threat to middle-class status may then explain the rise of populist nationalism in many parts of the world in the second decade of the twenty-first century.

In the United States, the working class, defined as people with a high school education or less, has not been doing well over the past generation. This is reflected not just in stagnant or declining incomes and job loss noted in the previous chapter, but in social breakdown as well. This began in the 1970s for the African-Americans who had migrated north in the years following World War II to cities such as Chicago, New York, and Detroit, where many of them were employed in the meat-packing, steel, or auto industries. As these sectors declined and men began to lose jobs through deindustrialization, a series of social ills followed, including rising crime rates, a crack cocaine epidemic, and deteriorating family life that helped transmit poverty from one generation to the next.[6]

Over the past decade, this kind of social deterioration spread to the white working class, as documented by two social scientists at opposite ends of the political spectrum, Charles Murray and Robert Putnam.[7] An opioid epidemic has broken out in rural and working-class communities that in 2016 led to more than sixty thousand deaths through drug overdoses, more than the number of Americans killed in traffic accidents each year. Life expectancies for white men have consequently fallen, something remarkable for a developed country.[8] The number of children growing up in single-parent families has significantly risen; the rate for white working-class children is now 35.6 percent.[9]

But perhaps one of the great drivers of the new American

nationalism that sent Donald Trump into the White House (and Britain out of the European Union) has been the perception of invisibility. Two recent studies of conservative voters in Wisconsin and Louisiana by Katherine Cramer and Arlie Hochschild, respectively, point to similar resentments. The overwhelmingly rural voters who supported Republican governor Scott Walker in Wisconsin explained that the elites in the capital, Madison, and in big cities outside the state simply did not understand them or pay attention to their problems. According to one of Cramer's interlocutors, Washington, D.C., "is a country unto itself . . . They haven't got a clue what the rest of the nation is up to, they're so absorbed in studying their own belly button."[10] Similarly, a Tea Party voter in rural Louisiana commented, "A lot of liberal commentators look down on people like me. We can't say the N-word. We wouldn't want to; it's demeaning. So why do liberal commentators feel so free to use the R-word [redneck]?"[11]

The resentful citizens fearing loss of middle-class status point an accusatory finger upward to the elites, to whom they are invisible, but also downward toward the poor, whom they feel are undeserving and being unfairly favored. According to Cramer, "resentment toward fellow citizens is front and center. People understand their circumstances as the fault of guilty and less deserving people, not as the product of broad social, economic, and political forces."[12] Hochschild presents a metaphor of ordinary people patiently waiting on a long line to get through a door labeled THE AMERICAN DREAM, and seeing other people suddenly cut in line ahead of them—African-Americans, women, immigrants—aided by those same elites who ignore them. "You are a stranger in your own land. You do not recognize yourself in how others see you. It is a struggle to feel seen and honored. And to feel honored you have to feel—

and feel seen as—moving forward. But through no fault of your own, and in ways that are hidden, you are slipping backward."[13]

Economic distress is often perceived by individuals not as resource deprivation, but as a loss of identity. Hard work should confer dignity on an individual, but that dignity is not recognized—indeed, it is condemned, and other people who are not willing to play by the rules are given undue advantages. This link between income and status helps to explain why nationalist or religious conservative groups have been more appealing to many people than traditional left-wing ones based on economic class. The nationalist can translate loss of relative economic position into loss of identity and status: you have always been a core member of our great nation, but foreigners, immigrants, and your own elite compatriots have been conspiring to hold you down; your country is no longer your own, and you are not respected in your own land. Similarly, the religious partisan can say something almost identical: You are a member of a great community of believers who have been traduced by nonbelievers; this betrayal has led not just to your impoverishment, but is a crime against God himself. You may be invisible to your fellow citizens, but you are not invisible to God.

This is why immigration has become such a neuralgic issue in many countries around the world. Immigration may or may not be helpful to a national economy: like trade, it is often of benefit in the aggregate, but does not benefit all groups within a society. However, it is almost always seen as a threat to cultural identity, especially when cross-border flows of people are as massive as they have been in recent decades. When economic decline is interpreted as loss of social status, it is easy to see why immigration becomes a proxy for economic change.

Yet this is not a fully satisfactory answer as to why the

nationalist right has in recent years captured voters who had formerly voted for parties of the left, both in the United States and in Europe. The latter has, after all, traditionally had a better practical answer to the economic dislocations caused by technological change and globalization with its broader social safety net. Moreover, progressives have in the past been able to appeal to communal identity, building it around a shared experience of exploitation and resentment of rich capitalists: "Workers of the world, unite!" "Stick it to the Man!" In the United States, working-class voters overwhelmingly supported the Democratic Party from the New Deal in the 1930s up until the rise of Ronald Reagan; European social democracy was built on a foundation of trade unionism and working-class solidarity.

The problem with the contemporary left is the particular forms of identity that it has increasingly chosen to celebrate. Rather than building solidarity around large collectivities such as the working class or the economically exploited, it has focused on ever smaller groups being marginalized in specific ways. This is part of a larger story about the fate of modern liberalism, in which the principle of universal and equal recognition has mutated into the special recognition of particular groups.

10

THE DEMOCRATIZATION OF DIGNITY

As we have seen, understandings of dignity forked in two directions during the nineteenth century, toward a liberal individualism that came to be embedded in the political rights of modern liberal democracies, and toward collective identities that could be defined by either nation or religion. Having taken a preliminary look at the collective understandings of identity, we will now return to the individualist ones—that is, identity as it has emerged in modern liberal democracies in North America and Europe.

In the latter group of countries, dignity has been democratized as political systems have progressively granted rights to wider and wider circles of individuals. At the time of the ratification of the U.S. Constitution in 1788, only white males with property had full political rights; the circle of rights bearers gradually expanded to include white men without property, African-Americans, indigenous people, and women. In this sense, liberal individualism gradually fulfilled its promise of becoming more democratic. But as it did so, it also evolved in a collective direction, such that the two strands ended up converging in surprising ways.

When we first encountered thymos and the desire for recognition of dignity in Plato's *Republic*, it was not generally shared among all human beings. Rather, it was the exclusive province of the guardian or warrior class, individuals who deserved recognition because of their willingness to risk their lives in a violent struggle to defend the larger community. We saw that dignity became universalized in the Christian tradition because all human beings were held to be capable of moral choice, a capacity that in Protestant thought was said to reside deep inside each individual. This concept of universal dignity was then secularized in the form of rational moral rules by Kant. To this, Rousseau added the idea that the inner moral self was not just capable of binary moral choices, but was filled with a plenitude of feelings and personal experiences that were suppressed by the surrounding society; access to those feelings rather than their suppression became the moral imperative. Dignity now centered on the recovery of the authentic inner being, and society's recognition of the potential that resided in each of its members. A liberal society increasingly came to be understood not just as a political order that protected certain minimal individual rights, but rather as one that actively encouraged the full actualization of the inner self.

In the Christian tradition, the inner self was the source of original sin, but was also the seat of moral choice by which sin could be overcome. Dignity rested on the ability of an individual believer to comply with a host of moral rules—regarding sex, the family, relations with neighbors and rulers—at the expense of inner sinful desires. With the erosion of the shared moral horizon established by common religion in Western countries, it became less possible to award dignity only to those individuals who complied with Christianity's moral rules. Religion was instead seen as a form of idolatry or false consciousness; recognition was due rather to the expressive inner self that might at times even want to transgress religious rules.

The way these ideas played out in twentieth-century American culture can be illustrated by the work of the California Task Force to Promote Self-Esteem and Personal Social Responsibility, which issued the report *Toward a State of Self-Esteem* in 1990. The task force was the brainchild of state legislator John Vasconcellos, who was influenced by the human potential movement that flourished in the California Bay Area from the 1960s on.[1] The latter built on the ideas of the psychologist Abraham Maslow, who became famous for his "hierarchy of needs." At the bottom of the hierarchy were basic physiological needs like food and drink; in the middle were social needs like safety and security; and at the top was something Maslow labeled "self-actualization." He argued that most people fail to realize the greater part of their potential; self-esteem was critical to self-actualization, since individuals were held back by low estimates of their own capabilities. Consistent with the modern concept of identity was the idea that the individual's self-actualization was a higher need than the requirements of the broader society.[2]

The task force defined self-esteem in the following terms:

Being alive as a human being has an innate importance, an importance to which the authors of the Declaration of Independence referred when they declared that all people "are endowed by their Creator with certain unalienable rights . . ." This conviction concerning the dignity of every human personality has long been part of our nation's moral and religious heritage. Every person has unique significance, simply because the precious and mysterious gift of life as a human being has been given. This is an inherent value which no adversary or adversity can take away.[3]

The report noted, "Appreciating my own worth and importance does not depend on measuring the quantity or quality of my abilities against those of someone else. Every person's abilities are valuable and needed. Each of us has a contribution to make to our society." It elaborated, "The point is not to become acceptable or worthy, but to acknowledge the worthiness that already exists. Our feelings are part of this, and accepting them builds our self-esteem . . . We each can celebrate our special race, ethnicity, and culture. We can appreciate our bodies, our gender, and our sexuality. We can accept our ideas, feelings, and creativity."[4]

In these few pages we can see the expression of a long line of ideas that ultimately trace back to Rousseau: that each of us has an inner self buried deep within; that it is unique and a source of creativity; that the self residing in each individual has an equal value to that of others; that the self is expressed not through reason but through feelings; and finally, that this inner self is the basis of the human dignity that is recognized in political documents such as the Declaration of Independence. It is, in short, a clear statement of the post-Rousseauian concept of identity.

The California task force report embodies a huge internal contradiction, however, which in turn reflects the fundamental tension between isothymia and megalothymia. It asserts that each individual has a creative and capable inner self. It strives to be nonjudgmental, warning that we should not compare ourselves to others or allow ourselves to be judged by other people's standards. However, the authors of the report quickly confront the problem that the inner selves we are celebrating may be cruel, violent, narcissistic, or dishonest. Or they may simply be lazy and shallow. Having affirmed the need for universal self-esteem, the report immediately states that self-esteem must also encompass "social responsibility" and "respect for others," noting that crime is the direct outcome of the absence of such respect. It celebrates, as a component of self-esteem, "integrity of character," which is composed of virtues such as "honesty, compassion, discipline, industriousness, reverence, perseverance, devotion, forgiveness, kindness, courage, gratitude, and grace." But not everyone is virtuous in these ways, which means that some people are more worthy of respect than others. We would never esteem a rapist or murderer as we would an upstanding citizen.

The view that self-esteem is based on an individual's ability to follow certain substantive social rules—to possess *virtues*—is a much more traditional understanding of human dignity. But since not everyone is virtuous, this understanding of esteem stands at odds with the report's desire to affirm everyone's intrinsic worth. This points to an inherent tension between isothymia and megalothymia. Megalothymia does not just reflect the vanity of the ambitious; it constitutes the just deserts of the virtuous. Some people need to be valued at a lower rate than others. Indeed, if one cannot feel shame—that is, low self-esteem—for having done bad things to other people, it is hard to see how one can ever come to accept responsibility for others. Nonetheless, the task force's report in two succeeding bullet points recommends that the state educational system simultaneously "serve to liberate rather than domesticate," and yet "promote responsible character and values." One can almost hear the liberal members of the task force arguing in the pages of the report for greater inclusiveness, the more conservative ones worrying about the consequences of this for social order, and the liberal ones responding in turn that "we can't be judgmental if we are to promote self-esteem."

The California task force report was widely mocked at the time, becoming the target of the *Doonesbury* comic strip for several months. The effort to raise everyone's self-esteem without being able to define what is estimable, and without being able to discriminate between better and worse forms of behavior, appeared to many people to be an impossible—indeed, an absurd—task. Yet in the succeeding years, this agenda took on a life of its own and became the objective of a large number of social institutions such as nonprofits, schools, and universities, and of the state itself. One reason that identity politics has become so embedded in the United States and other liberal democracies is because of rising concern over self-esteem, and by what has been labeled "the triumph of the therapeutic."

The latter refers to a 1966 book written by the sociologist Philip Rieff, who argued that the decline of a shared moral horizon defined by religion had left a huge void that was being filled by psychologists preaching a new religion of psychotherapy. Traditional culture, according to Rieff, "is another name for a design of motive directing the self outward, toward those communal purposes in which alone the self can be realized and satisfied." As such it played a therapeutic role, giving purpose to individuals, connecting them to others, and teaching them their place in the universe. But that outer culture had been denounced as an iron cage imprisoning the inner self; people were told to liberate their inner selves, to be "authentic" and "committed," but without being told to what they should be committed. The void left by priests and ministers was now being filled by psychoanalysts using therapeutic techniques "with nothing at stake beyond a manipulatable sense of well-being."[5] Rieff's critique of the therapeutic spawned an entire genre of social commentary in the next generation whose target was the modern model of identity itself.[6]

The original therapeutic model was built around the discovery of hidden identity. Sigmund Freud came to his psychological insights treating Viennese women crippled by what he labeled hysteria, an intense unconscious repression of their natural sexuality, driven by what Freud would come to call the superego. Freud's account of the inner self shifted over time, from memories of childhood abuse to projected sexual fantasies; in either case, therapy rested on the recovery of knowledge of the provenance of the person's condition. Freud remained morally neutral in the standoff between the inner self and the demands of society, recognizing that both had powerful claims; if anything, he was on the side of society. But he was part of an "unmasking trend," in Lionel Trilling's words, founded on the belief that "beneath the appearance of every human phenomenon there lies concealed a discrepant actuality and that intellectual, practical and (not least) moral advantage is to be gained by forcibly bringing it to light."[7] Many of Freud's followers, such as Herbert Marcuse, and those in subsequent psychiatric traditions, were less neutral than Freud and saw their role as that of liberators of the individual against a broadly repressive society.

The affirmation of inner identity depended, in the final analysis, on the truth of Rousseau's assertion that human beings were fundamentally good: that their inner selves were sources of limitless potential (what Rousseau called perfectibility), and that human happiness depended on the liberation of that self from artificial social constraint. That was certainly the starting assumption of the human potential movement and the California task force.

But what if Rousseau was wrong and that inner self was, as traditional moralists believed, the seat of asocial or harmful impulses, indeed of evil? Some in the human potential movement saw Friedrich Nietzsche as one of their progenitors. But Nietzsche was ruthlessly honest in foreseeing the consequences of personal liberation: it could just as easily pave the way for a post-Christian morality in which the stronger ruled the weaker, rather than a happy egalitarian outcome. Adolf Hitler would end up doing nothing more than following his inner star, as countless college graduates are constantly enjoined to do.

This was exactly the critique made in the late 1970s by Christopher Lasch, who argued that the promotion of self-esteem enabled not human potential but a crippling narcissism, indeed, a narcissism that he felt had come to characterize American society as a whole. People were not liberated to fulfill their potential; rather, they were trapped in emotional dependence: "Notwithstanding his occasional illusions of omnipotence, the narcissist depends on others to validate his self-esteem. He cannot live without an admiring audience." This had hugely negative social implications:

> Even when therapists speak of the need for "meaning" and "love," they define love and meaning simply as the fulfillment of the patient's emotional requirements. It hardly occurs to them—nor is there any reason why it should, given the nature of the therapeutic enterprise—to encourage the subject to subordinate his needs and interests to those of others, to some cause or tradition outside himself.

In an American context, Lasch argued that narcissism as a social phenomenon would lead not to fascism, but to a broad depoliticization of society, in which struggles for social justice were reduced to personal psychological problems.[8] Lasch wrote well before the rise of Donald Trump, a political figure who almost perfectly embodies the narcissism he describes. Narcissism led Trump into politics, but a politics driven less by public purposes than his own inner needs for public affirmation.

Moralists such as Rieff and Lasch may have been right about the social consequences of a therapeutic society. But by the time they wrote, an entire psychiatric profession had arisen, whose members did not see themselves simply as scientists observing natural phenomena; they were also doctors with a therapeutic calling to heal their patients and make them more functional. Ordinary people who wanted to feel better about themselves created a huge demand for their services. Freudian psychoanalysis in the last decades of the twentieth century went into a long-term decline in the United States, but the underlying therapeutic model continued to gain ground, and psychological language began to permeate the popular culture of developed societies. For example, the term *self-esteem* was virtually absent from U.K. newspapers in 1980, but references to low self-esteem began to rise steadily to well over thirty-three hundred by the year 2000. Psychological counseling expanded, with a fourfold increase in the number of mental health professionals between 1970 and 1995.[9]

If therapy became a substitute for religion, religion itself took an increasingly therapeutic turn. This was true of both liberal and evangelical churches in the United States, whose leaders found that they could reverse the trend toward declining attendance if they offered what amounted to psychological counseling services built around self-esteem. Robert Schuller, a prominent televangelist whose *Hour of Power* show was broadcast weekly to millions of viewers over several decades, and whose Crystal Cathedral in Garden Grove, California, was one of the largest churches in the United States, wrote a book early on entitled *Self-Esteem: The New Reformation*.[10] Rick Warren, whose Church Growth Movement has transformed many thousands of evangelical churches in recent decades, has put forth a similar therapeutic message. His trademarked Purpose Driven Life movement emphasizes the importance of pastors attending to the "felt needs" of nonbelievers, deemphasizing traditional Christian doctrine in favor of an overtly psychological language. Like Schuller, and like the California task force, he downplays sin and any judgmental aspect of traditional religion; the Gospel is more of an "owner's manual" for how to achieve happiness in this life rather than in the one beyond.[11] Luther's Christian dignity was something hard to achieve; the Purpose Driven Life by contrast is available to everyone.

The therapeutic turn in the popular culture of advanced liberal democracies such as the United States was inevitably reflected in its politics, and in an evolving understanding of the role of the state. In the classical liberalism of the nineteenth century, the state was held responsible for protecting basic rights such as freedom of speech and association, for upholding a rule of law, and for providing essential public services such as police, roads, and education. The government "recognized" its citizens by granting them individual rights, but the state was not seen as responsible for making each individual feel better about himself or herself.

Under the therapeutic model, however, an individual's happiness depends on his or her self-esteem, and self-esteem is a by-product of public recognition. Governments are readily able to give away public recognition in the way that they talk about and treat their citizens, so modern liberal societies naturally and perhaps inevitably began to take on the responsibility for raising the self-esteem of each and every one of their citizens. We noted already Supreme Court justice Kennedy's opinion that liberty was not simply freedom from government action, but "the right to define one's own concept of existence, of meaning, of the universe, and of the mystery of human life," a view that could have come directly out of the Esalen Institute.

Therapeutic services came to be deeply embedded in social policy, not just in California but throughout the United States and in other liberal democracies. States began to offer psychological counseling and other mental health services, and schools began to incorporate therapeutic insights into the way that they taught children. This expansion took place in stages, in tandem with the growth of the American welfare state from the New Deal onward. In the early twentieth century, social dysfunctions such as delinquency or teen pregnancy were seen as deviant behavior that needed to be dealt with punitively, often through the criminal justice system. But with the rise of therapeutic approaches by midcentury, they were increasingly seen as social pathologies that needed to be treated through counseling and psychiatric intervention. The 1956 amendments to the Social Security Act allowed for federal reimbursements of a range of therapeutic services to strengthen family life and self-support. These subsidies were further enhanced by new amendments in 1962, leading to an explosion of caseworkers and caseloads in the following decade. Title XX amendments in 1974 broadened the coverage beyond the poor to middle-class recipients.[12]

This rapid expansion of therapeutic social services triggered a conservative backlash in the Nixon and Reagan administrations, along with efforts to cut their growth. Yet by then therapeutic responses to life problems were demanded by millions of ordinary people, who were now less comfortable turning to pastors, parents, companies, or other traditional sources of authority. The therapeutic state metastasized across a wide number of institutions, including a large nonprofit sector that by the 1990s had become the delivery vehicle for state-funded social services.[13]

Universities found themselves at the forefront of the therapeutic revolution. This can be illustrated by the controversy that broke out in 1987 over Stanford University's Western Culture core course. That year civil rights leader the Reverend Jesse Jackson led a group of Stanford students in chanting, "Hey, hey, ho, ho, Western Culture's got to go"—which earned the university instant national attention. The existing core course was built around fifteen texts, beginning with the Hebrew Bible, Homer, and Augustine, continuing through Machiavelli and Galileo, and on to Marx, Darwin, and Freud. The protesters wanted to expand the syllabus to include nonwhite and female authors, not necessarily on the grounds that they wrote important or timeless books, but that their very inclusion raised the dignity of the cultures out of which they came, and therefore the self-esteem of students coming from those cultures.

The therapeutic motive underlying demands for changes in the curriculum was evident in the testimony given by Bill King, president of Stanford's Black Student Union, in the original debate over Western Culture:

> I know Professors . . . are simply preserving that tradition which they consider correct . . . But by focusing these ideas on all of us they are crushing the psyche of those others to whom Locke, Hume, and Plato are not speaking, and they are denying the freshmen and women a chance to broaden their

perspective to accept both Hume and Imhotep, Machiavelli and Al Malgili, Rousseau and Mary Wollstonecraft . . . The Western culture program as it is presently structured around a core list and an outdated philosophy of the West being Greece, Europe, and Euro-America is wrong, and worse, it hurts people mentally and emotionally in ways that are not even recognized.[14]

What is revealing about King's statement is that his justification for the curricular shift is entirely psychological: the current canon is "crushing the psyche" of minority and female students, and hurting people "mentally and emotionally in ways that are not even recognized." A wider reading list will not necessarily transmit valuable or timeless knowledge that would be educationally important; rather, it would raise the self-esteem of marginalized students and make them feel better about themselves.[15]

The therapeutic model arose directly from modern understandings of identity. It held that we have deep interior spaces whose potentialities are not being realized, and that external society through its rules, roles, and expectations is responsible for holding us back. This requires both an individual plumbing of that inner space and a potentially revolutionary agenda to liberate us from the restraining rules. The therapist was not particularly interested in the substantive content of what was inside us, nor in the abstract question of whether the surrounding society was just or unjust. The therapist is simply interested in making his or her patients feel better about themselves, which required raising their sense of self-worth.

The rise of the therapeutic model midwifed the birth of modern identity politics in advanced liberal democracies. Identity politics is everywhere a struggle for the recognition of dignity. Liberal democracies are premised on the equal recognition of the dignity of each of their citizens *as individuals.* Over time, the sphere of equal recognition has expanded both quantitatively, in the numbers of people accepted as rights-bearing citizens, and qualitatively, in an evolving understanding of recognition not just as formal rights but as substantive self-esteem.

Dignity was being democratized. But identity politics in liberal democracies began to reconverge with the collective and illiberal forms of identity such as nation and religion, since individuals frequently wanted not recognition of their individuality, but recognition of their sameness to other people.

11

FROM IDENTITY TO IDENTITIES

The 1960s witnessed the emergence of a series of powerful new social movements across the world's developed liberal democracies. In the United States, the civil rights movement demanded that the country fulfill the promise of racial equality in the Declaration of Independence and written into the Constitution at the end of the Civil War. This was soon followed by the feminist movement, which similarly sought equal treatment for women, a cause that both stimulated and was shaped by a massive influx of women into the labor market. A parallel sexual revolution shattered traditional norms regarding sexuality and the family, and an environmental movement reshaped attitudes toward humanity's relationship with nature. Subsequent years would see the emergence of other movements promoting the rights of the disabled, Native Americans, immigrants, gays, lesbians, and eventually transgender people.

Europe saw a similar explosion following the *événements* in France in May 1968. The old French left was formed around a nucleus of hard-core Communists, whose sympathizers included famous intellectuals such as Jean-Paul Sartre. Their agenda remained focused on the industrial working class and Marxist revolution. In the 1968 uprisings, those preoccupations were displaced by many of the same social issues that were roiling the United States: the rights of minorities and immigrants, the status of women, environmentalism, and the like. Proletarian revolution no longer seemed relevant to the issues facing contemporary Europe. The student protests and widespread strikes that took place across France echoed similar developments in Germany, the Netherlands, Scandinavia, and other places. This "generation of 1968" on the left was no longer focused single-mindedly on class struggle, but rather on support for the rights of a broad range of marginalized groups.

These social movements emerged as they did out of the aspiration of liberal democracies to recognize equally the dignity of all citizens. But democracies never live up to this pretension: people are often judged not on their individual character and abilities, whatever the law says, but on assumptions about them as members of groups.

In the United States, these prejudices were, shamefully, reflected for many years in formal laws that did not allow black children to be educated together with white ones, or that denied women the vote on the grounds that they were insufficiently rational. But even when those laws were changed to desegregate schools and enfranchise women, the broader society did not suddenly cease thinking of itself in group terms. The psychological burdens of discrimination, prejudice, disrespect, or simple invisibility remained ingrained in social consciousness. They also remained because groups continued to differ from one another in their behavior, performance, wealth, traditions, and customs.

The new social movements that appeared in the 1960s arose in societies already primed to think in identity terms, and whose institutions had taken on the therapeutic mission of raising people's self-esteem. Up until the 1960s, concern with identity had largely been the province of those who wanted to actualize their individual potentialities. But with the rise of these social movements, many people naturally came to think of their own aims and objectives in terms of the dignity of the groups of which they were members. Research on ethnic movements around the world has shown that individual self-esteem is related to the esteem conferred on the larger group with which one is associated; thus the political would affect the personal.[1] Each movement represented people who had up to then been invisible and suppressed; each resented that invisibility and wanted public recognition of their inner worth. So was born what we today label as modern identity politics. Only the term was new; these groups were replicating the struggles and perspectives of earlier nationalist and religious identity movements.

Each marginalized group had a choice of seeing itself in broader or narrower identity terms. It could demand that society treat its members identically to the way that the dominant groups in society were treated, or it could assert a separate identity for its members and demand respect for them as *different* from the mainstream society. Over time, the latter strategy tended to win out. The early civil rights movement of Dr. Martin Luther King, Jr., simply demanded that American society treat black people the way it treated white people. It didn't attack the norms and values that governed the way white people dealt with one another or demand that the country's basic democratic institutions change. By the end of the 1960s, however, groups such as the Black Panthers or the Nation of Islam emerged that argued that black people had their own traditions and consciousness; black people needed to take pride in themselves for what they were and not for what the broader society wanted them to be. In the words of the poem written by William Holmes Borders, Sr., and recited by the Reverend Jesse Jackson, "I may be poor, but I am—Somebody!" The authentic inner selves of black Americans were not those of white people, but were shaped by the unique experiences of growing up black in a hostile white society. This experience was defined by violence, racism, and denigration and could not be appreciated by people who grew up differently.

These themes have been taken up in today's Black Lives Matter movement, which arose in response to police violence in Ferguson (Missouri), Baltimore, New York, and other American cities. This movement broadened over time from a demand for justice for individual victims such as Michael Brown or Eric Garner, to an effort to make people aware of the nature of day-to-day existence for black Americans. Writers such as Ta-Nehisi Coates have connected contemporary police violence against African-Americans to the long historical memory of slavery and lynching. This memory constitutes part of a gulf of understanding between blacks and whites based on their different lived experiences.[2]

The same evolution occurred within the feminist movement, only more quickly and powerfully. The demands of the mainstream movement were focused, like the early civil rights movement, on equal treatment for women in employment, education, the courts, and so on. But from the beginning an important strand of feminist thought argued that the consciousness and life experiences of women were fundamentally different from those of men, and that the movement's aim should not simply be to facilitate women's behaving and thinking like men. Simone de Beauvoir's highly influential 1949 book, *The Second Sex*, asserted that women's experience of life and their bodies was heavily shaped by the patriarchal nature of the society around them, and that this experience could be scarcely perceived by men.[3] This view was expressed in a more extreme form by feminist legal scholar Catharine MacKinnon, who argued that rape and intercourse were "difficult to distinguish," and that existing laws on rape reflected the rapist's point of view. While not all of the writers of such laws were rapists, she said, "they are a member of the group who do [rape] and who do for reasons that they share in common even with those who don't, namely masculinity and their identification with masculine norms."[4]

The idea that each group has its own identity that was not accessible to outsiders was reflected in the use of the term *lived experience*, which has seen explosive growth in the popular culture since the 1970s.[5] The distinction between *experience* and *lived experience* has its roots in the difference between the German words *Erfahrung* and *Erlebnis*, which preoccupied a number of thinkers in the nineteenth century. *Erfahrung* referred to experiences that could be shared, as when people witnessed chemistry experiments in different laboratories. *Erlebnis* (which incorporates the word *Leben*, or "life"), by contrast, meant the subjective perception of experiences, which might not necessarily be shareable. The writer Walter Benjamin argued in a 1939 essay that modern life constituted a series of "shock experiences" that prevented individuals from seeing their lives as a whole and made it hard to convert *Erlebnis* into *Erfahrung*. He saw this negatively as a "new kind of barbarism" in which communal memory breaks down into a series of individual experiences.[6] This line of thought ultimately traces back, we should recall, to Jean-Jacques Rousseau, whose emphasis on the "sentiment of existence" valorized subjective inner feeling over the shared norms and understandings of the surrounding society.

The distinction between *Erfahrung* and *Erlebnis* is the same as the distinction between *experience* and *lived experience*. The latter term entered the English language via Simone de Beauvoir: the second volume of *The Second Sex* was entitled *L'expérience vécue*, or "lived experience." The lived experience of women was not the lived experience of men, she argued. Women's subjective experiences raised the profile of subjectivity as such, which was applied to other groups and categories: those based on race, ethnicity, gender orientation, disability, and the like. Within each of these categories, lived experiences were different: those of gays and lesbians differ from those of transgender people; a black man in Baltimore has a different experience from a black woman in Birmingham, Alabama.

The new prominence of lived experience reflects the broader nature of long-term modernization, one we noted earlier that gave rise to the problem of identity in the first place. Modernization entails the emergence of a complex society with an elaborate division of labor, the personal mobility that necessarily underlies modern market economies, and the movement from village to city that creates a diverse pluralism of individuals living next to one another. In contemporary societies, these social changes were deepened by modern communications technology and social media, which allow like-minded individuals in geographically separate places to communicate with one another. In such a world, lived experiences, and therefore identities, begin to proliferate exponentially, just like YouTube stars and Facebook circles on the internet. What erodes just as rapidly is the possibility of old-fashioned "experience," that is, perspectives and feelings that can be shared across group boundaries.

The therapeutic turn that institutions such as schools, universities, health centers, and other social services had taken meant that they were ready to minister to people's psyches—the isothymia driving each social movement—as well as to their material conditions. As the growing consciousness of racial minorities and women became stronger in the seventies and eighties, a vocabulary and framework were ready-made for understanding their experiences of marginalization. Identity, which had formerly been a matter for individuals, now became the property of groups that were seen as having their own cultures shaped by their own lived experiences.

Multiculturalism was a description of societies that were de facto diverse. But it also became the label for a political program that sought to value each separate culture and each lived experience equally, and in particular those that had been invisible or undervalued in the past. While classical liberalism sought to protect the autonomy of equal individuals, the new ideology of multiculturalism promoted equal respect for cultures, even if those cultures abridged the autonomy of the individuals who participated in them.

Multiculturalism was originally used in reference to large cultural groups such as Canadian francophones or Muslim immigrants or African-Americans. But these groups fragmented further into smaller and more specific groups with distinct experiences, as well as groups defined by the intersection of different forms of discrimination, such as women of color, whose lives could not be understood through the lens of either race or gender alone.[7]

Another factor driving the shift of focus to identity was the increasing difficulty of crafting policies that would bring about large-scale socioeconomic change. By the 1970s and '80s, progressive groups were facing an existential crisis throughout the developed world. The hard left had been defined for the first half of the century by Marxism and the Marxist emphasis on the working class and the proletarian revolution. The social democratic left, which unlike the Marxists accepted liberal democracy as a framework, had a different agenda: it sought to expand the welfare state to cover more people with more social protections. In both its Marxist and its social democratic variants, the left hoped to increase socioeconomic equality through the use of state power, both to open access to social services to all citizens and to redistribute wealth and income.

The limits of this strategy were evident as the century drew to a close. The Marxist left had to confront the fact that actual Communist societies in the Soviet Union and China had turned into grotesque and oppressive dictatorships, denounced by leaders such as Nikita Khrushchev and Mikhail Gorbachev, who were themselves Communists. Meanwhile the working class in most industrialized democracies grew richer and began to merge happily with the middle class. Communist revolution and the abolition of private property fell off the agenda.

The social democratic left also reached a dead end of sorts: its goals of an ever-expanding welfare state bumped into the reality of fiscal constraints during the turbulent 1970s. Governments responded by printing money, leading to inflation and financial crisis; redistributive programs were creating perverse incentives that discouraged work, savings, and entrepreneurship, which in turn limited the size of the pie available for redistribution. Inequality remained deeply entrenched, despite ambitious efforts such as Lyndon Johnson's Great Society to eradicate it. With the collapse of the Soviet Union in 1991 and

China's shift toward a market economy after 1978, the Marxist left largely collapsed, and social democrats were left to make their peace with capitalism. The left also came to share with the right an increasing disillusionment with government itself after failures such as the Vietnam War and the Watergate scandal.

The diminished ambitions for large-scale socioeconomic reform converged with the left's embrace of identity politics and multiculturalism in the final decades of the twentieth century. The left continued to be defined by its passion for equality, but that agenda shifted from its earlier emphasis on the conditions of the working class to the often psychological demands of an ever-widening circle of marginalized groups. Many activists came to see the old working class and their trade unions as a privileged stratum with little sympathy for the plight of groups such as immigrants or racial minorities worse off than they were. Recognition struggles targeted newer groups and their rights as groups, rather than the economic inequality of individuals. In the process, the old working class was left behind.

Something similar happened in European countries such as France, where the hard left had always been more prominent than in the United States. After the *événements* of May 1968, the revolutionary goals of the old Marxist left no longer seemed relevant to the new Europe that was emerging. The left's agenda shifted to culture: what needed to be smashed was not the current political order that exploited the working class, but the hegemony of Western culture and values that suppressed minorities at home and developing countries abroad.[8] Classical Marxism had accepted many of the underpinnings of the Western Enlightenment: a belief in science and rationality, in historical progress, and in the superiority of modern societies over traditional ones. By contrast, the new cultural left was more Nietzschean and relativistic, attacking the Christian and democratic values on which the Western Enlightenment had been based. Western culture was seen as the incubator of colonialism, patriarchy, and environmental destruction. This critique then filtered back into the United States as postmodernism and deconstructionism in American universities.

Europeans became more multicultural, both in fact and as a matter of principle. Immigrant communities, often heavily Muslim, grew in many European countries in response to early post–World War II labor shortages. In the early days, activists in these communities pushed for equal rights for immigrants and their children, but found themselves frustrated by continuing barriers to upward mobility and social integration. Inspired both by the 1979 Iranian Revolution and by Saudi support for Salafist mosques and madrassas, Islamist groups began to appear in Europe that argued that Muslims should not seek to integrate, but should maintain separate cultural institutions. Many people on the European left embraced this trend, regarding Islamists as more authentic spokesmen for the marginalized than westernized Muslims who had chosen to integrate into the social system.[9] In France, Muslims became the new proletariat, with part of the left abandoning its traditional secularism in the name of cultural pluralism. Criticisms that Islamists were themselves intolerant and illiberal were often downplayed under the banner of antiracism and countering Islamophobia.

The shifting agenda by the progressive left in the United States and Europe had both advantages and drawbacks. The embrace of identity politics was both understandable and necessary. The lived experiences of identity groups are different from one another and often need to be addressed in ways specific to those groups. Outsiders to those groups often fail to perceive the harm they are doing by their actions, as many men realized in the wake of the #MeToo movement's highlighting of sexual harassment and sexual assault. Identity politics aims at changing culture and behavior in ways that will have real benefits for the people involved.

By turning a spotlight on narrower experiences of injustice, identity politics has brought about welcome changes in concrete public policies that have benefited the groups in question, as well as in cultural norms. The Black Lives Matter movement has made police departments across the United States much more conscious of the way they treat minority citizens, even if cases of police abuse still continue. The #MeToo movement has broadened popular understanding of sexual assault, and has opened an important discussion of the inadequacies of existing criminal law in dealing with it. Its most important consequence is probably the broad normative shift that it has already brought about in the way that women and men interact in workplaces around the United States and beyond.

So there is nothing wrong with identity politics as such; it is a natural and inevitable response to injustice. It becomes problematic only when identity is interpreted or asserted in certain specific ways. Identity politics for some progressives has become a cheap substitute for serious thinking about how to reverse the thirty-year trend in most liberal democracies toward greater socioeconomic inequality. It is easier to argue over cultural issues within the confines of elite institutions than it is to appropriate money or convince skeptical legislators to change policies. The most visible manifestations of identity politics have appeared on university campuses from the 1980s onward. University curricula can be more readily altered to include readings of women and minority authors than can the incomes or social situations of the groups in question. Many of the constituencies that have been the focus of recent identity claims, such as female executives in Silicon Valley or aspiring women actresses and filmmakers in Hollywood, are near the top of the income distribution. Helping them to achieve greater equality is a good thing, but will do nothing to address the glaring disparities between the top 1 percent and the remaining 99.

This points to a second problem that arises with a focus on newer and more narrowly defined marginalized groups: it diverts attention from older and larger groups whose serious problems have been ignored. A significant part of the white American working class has been dragged into an underclass, comparable to the experience of African-Americans during the 1970s and '80s. Yet one has heard little concern from activists on the left, at least until recently, about the burgeoning opioid crisis, or the fate of children growing up in impoverished single-parent families in the rural United States. Progressives today have no ambitious strategies for dealing with the potentially immense job losses that will accompany advancing automation, or the income disparities that technology may bring to all Americans, white or black, male or female. The same problem afflicts parties of the left in Europe: the French Communist and Socialist parties have lost significant numbers of voters to the National Front in recent decades, while the German Social Democrats' embrace of Angela Merkel's welcome of Syrian refugees led to similar defections in the 2017 elections.[10]

A third problem with current understandings of identity is that they can threaten free speech and, more broadly, the kind of rational discourse needed to sustain a democracy. Liberal democracies are committed to protecting the right to say anything you want in a marketplace of ideas, particularly in the political sphere. But the preoccupation with identity has clashed with the need for deliberative discourse. The focus on lived experience by identity groups valorizes inner selves experienced

emotionally rather than examined rationally. Notes one ob-
server, "Our political culture is marked, at the micro level, by
the fusion of a given person's opinion and what they perceive
to be their singular, permanent, and authentic self." This privi-
leges opinions sincerely held over reasoned deliberation that
may force one to abandon those opinions.[11] That an argument
is offensive to someone's sense of self-worth is often seen as sufficient to delegitimize it, a trend encouraged by the kind of
short-form discourse propagated by social media.[12]

The political strategy of building a left out of a coalition of
disparate identity groups is problematic as well, as Mark Lilla
has explained.[13] The current dysfunction and decay of the
American political system is related to the extreme and ever-
growing polarization of American politics, which has made
routine governing an exercise in brinkmanship and threatens
to politicize all of the country's institutions. The blame for
this polarization is not equally shared between left and right.
As Thomas Mann and Norman Ornstein have argued, the Republican Party has moved much more rapidly toward the extremist views represented by its Tea Party wing than has the
Democratic Party to its left.[14] But the left has moved further to
the left as well. In doing so, both parties are responding to the
incentives that a two-party electoral system and popular pri-
maries give to politically conscious activists. The activists most
concerned with identity issues are seldom broadly representative of the electorate as a whole; indeed, their concerns have
often alienated mainstream voters. Moreover, the very nature of
modern identity with its emphasis on lived experiences creates
conflicts *within* the liberal coalition. For example, controversies
over "cultural appropriation" have set progressive blacks and
whites against one another.[15]

The final, and perhaps most significant, problem with

identity politics as currently practiced on the left is that it has stimulated the rise of identity politics on the right. Identity politics gives rise to *political correctness*, opposition to which has become a major source of mobilization on the right. Since the latter term became a central issue in the 2016 U.S. presidential election, it is necessary to step back a bit and think about the origins of the phrase.

Political correctness refers to things you can't say in public without fearing withering moral opprobrium. Every society has certain ideas that run counter to its foundational ideas of legitimacy and therefore are off-limits in public discourse. In a liberal democracy, one is free to believe and say in private that Hitler was right to kill the Jews, or that slavery was a benevolent institution. Under the U.S. First Amendment, one's right to say these sorts of things is also constitutionally protected. But considerable moral opprobrium would rightly be brought to bear against any political figure espousing such views, since they run counter to the principle of equality enunciated in the American Declaration of Independence. In many European democracies that do not have the same absolutist view of free speech as the United States, similar statements have been criminalized for many years.

But the social phenomenon of political correctness is more complex than this. The constant discovery of new identities and the shifting grounds for acceptable speech are hard to follow: *manholes* are now referred to as *maintenance holes*; the name of the Washington Redskins football team is denigrating to Native Americans; the use of *he* or *she* in the wrong context denotes insensitivity to intersex or transgender people. The eminent biologist E. O. Wilson once had a bucket of water dumped on his head for suggesting that some gender differences had biological grounds. None of these words have any significance for fundamental democratic principles; what they do is challenge the dignity of a particular group and denote lack of awareness of or sympathy for that group's particular challenges and struggles.

The more extreme forms of political correctness are in the end the province of relatively small numbers of writers, artists, students, and intellectuals on the left. But they are picked up by the conservative media and amplified as representative of the left as a whole. This may then explain one of the extraordinary aspects of the 2016 U.S. presidential election, which is Donald Trump's continuing popularity among a core group of supporters despite behavior that would have ended the career of any other politician. In his campaign he mocked a disabled journalist; he was revealed to have bragged that he had groped women; and he characterized Mexicans as rapists and criminals. While many of his supporters may not have approved of each individual statement, they liked the fact that he was not intimidated by the pressure to be politically correct. Trump was the perfect practitioner of the ethics of authenticity that defines our age: he may be mendacious, malicious, bigoted, and unpresidential, but at least he says what he thinks.

By taking on political correctness so frontally, Trump has played a critical role in moving the focus of identity politics from the left, where it was born, to the right, where it is now taking root. Identity politics on the left tended to legitimate only certain identities while ignoring or denigrating others, such as European (i.e., white) ethnicity, Christian religiosity, rural residence, belief in traditional family values, and related categories. Many of Donald Trump's working-class supporters feel they have been disregarded by the national elites. Hollywood makes movies with strong female, black, or gay characters, but few centering around people like themselves, except occasionally to make fun of them (think of Will Ferrell's *Talladega Nights*). Rural people, who are the backbone of populist movements not just in the United States but in Britain, Hungary, Poland, and other countries, often believe that their traditional values are under severe threat by cosmopolitan, city-based elites. They feel victimized by a secular culture that is careful not to criticize Islam or Judaism, yet regards their own Christianity as a mark of bigotry. They feel that the elite media have put them in danger by their political correctness, as when the mainstream German press failed to report for several days an incident of mass groping and sexual assault by a crowd of mostly Muslim men at a 2016 New Year's celebration in Cologne, all for fear of stoking Islamophobia.

The most dangerous of these new right-wing identities are those related to race. President Trump has been careful not to articulate overtly racist views. But he has happily accepted support from individuals and groups that hold them. As a candidate he was evasive in criticizing the former Ku Klux Klan leader David Duke and, after the August 2017 "Unite the Right" gathering in Charlottesville, Virginia, laid blame for the violence on "both sides." He has spent a lot of time singling out black athletes and celebrities for criticism. The country has become further polarized over whether to remove statues honoring Confederate heroes, an issue Trump has been happy to exploit. Since his rise, white nationalism has moved from a fringe movement to something much more mainstream in American politics. Its proponents argue that it has been politically acceptable to talk about Black Lives Matter or gay rights or Latino voters as groups that can legitimately organize around a specific identity. But if one even uses the adjective *white* as self-identification or, worse yet, organizes politically around the theme of "white rights," one is immediately identified, the white nationalists note, as a racist and bigot.

Similar things are happening in other liberal democracies. White nationalism has a long history in Europe, where it was called fascism. Fascism was defeated militarily in 1945 and has been carefully suppressed ever since. But recent events have loosened some of the restraints. As a result of the refugee crisis of the mid-2010s, a panic has arisen in Eastern Europe over the possibility that Muslim migrants might shift the region's demographic balance. In November 2017, on the anniversary of Poland's independence, an estimated sixty thousand people marched through Warsaw chanting "Pure Poland, white Poland" and "Refugees get out!" (This was despite Poland's being home to a relatively small number of refugees.) The ruling populist Law and Justice Party distanced itself from the demonstrators, but, like Donald Trump, sent mixed signals that suggested it was not entirely unsympathetic to the aims of the marchers.[16]

The proponents of identity politics on the left would argue that assertions of identity on the right are illegitimate and cannot be placed on the same moral plane as those of minorities, women, and other marginalized groups. Rather, they reflect the perspectives of a dominant mainstream culture that has been historically privileged and continues to be so.

These arguments have obvious truth. Perceptions on the part of conservatives of advantages being unfairly given to minorities, women, or refugees are greatly exaggerated, as is the sense that political correctness has run amok everywhere. Social media contributes heavily to this problem, since a single comment or incident can ricochet around the internet and become emblematic of an entire category of people. The reality for many marginalized groups continues as before: African-Americans continue to be objects of police violence, and women continue to be assaulted and harassed.

What is notable, however, is how the right has adopted the language and framing of identity from the left: the idea that my particular group is being victimized, that its situation and sufferings are invisible to the rest of society, and that the whole of the social and political structure responsible for this situation (read: the media and political elites) needs to be smashed. Identity politics is the lens through which most social issues are now seen across the ideological spectrum.

Liberal democracies have good reasons not to organize themselves around a series of ever-proliferating identity groups inaccessible to outsiders. The dynamic of identity politics is to stimulate more of the same, as identity groups begin to see one another as threats. Unlike fights over economic resources, identity claims are usually nonnegotiable: rights to social recognition based on race, ethnicity, or gender are based on fixed biological characteristics and cannot be traded for other goods or abridged in any way.

Despite the beliefs of certain advocates on both the left and the right, identities are not biologically determined; while they are shaped by experience and environment, they can be defined in terms that are either tightly focused or broad. That I am born a certain way does not mean I have to think in a certain way; lived experience can eventually be translated into shared experience. Societies need to protect the marginalized and excluded, but they also need to achieve common goals via deliberation and consensus. The shift in agendas of both left and right toward the protection of ever narrower group identities ultimately threatens the possibility of communication and collective action. The remedy for this is not to abandon the idea of identity, which is too much a part of the way that modern people think about themselves and their surrounding societies. The remedy is to define larger and more integrative national identities that take account of the de facto diversity of existing liberal democratic societies. This will be the subject of the two following chapters.

12

WE THE PEOPLE

In the wake of the 2011 Arab Spring, Syria descended into a devastating civil war that has left an estimated 400,000 people dead. According to the UN High Commissioner for Refugees, 4.8 million people have fled the country, including 1 million going to Europe, and another 6.6 million have been displaced within Syria—this in a country that had a population of 18 million at the start of the conflict. The knock-on consequences of this war include destabilization of the politics of Syria's neighbors Turkey, Jordan, Lebanon, and Iraq, and a migrant crisis that has rocked the European Union.

Syria is an extreme example of what happens when a country lacks a clear sense of national identity. The proximate cause of the war were peaceful protests that broke out in 2011 against the regime of Bashar al-Assad, which were triggered by the Arab Spring. Rather than stepping down, Assad met his opponents with fierce repression. The latter then responded with violence themselves, and the conflict began to attract the attention of outside groups, with foreign fighters streaming in to join ISIS. The civil war was further deepened by support from Turkey, Saudi Arabia, Iran, Russia, and the United States.

Underlying these events were the realities of sectarian division. Following a coup in 1970, Syria was ruled by Hafiz al-Assad and, after 2000, by his son Bashar, who were members of the Alawite sect. The Alawites, a branch of Shia Islam, constituted perhaps 12 percent of Syria's prewar population; the majority of the remainder were Sunni Muslims, with significant Christian, Yazidi, and other minority populations. There were also ethnic and linguistic divisions between Arabs, Kurds, Druze, Turkmen, Palestinians, Circassians, and the like, which sometimes also corresponded to religious fractures. Ideological divisions also existed between violent extremists, moderate Islamists, leftists, and liberals. The Alawites had come to dominate Syrian political life because they had been recruited into the military by the French under a divide-and-rule strategy when the latter were the region's colonial masters. Throughout the Assad family's rule, the Alawites were hated and resisted by other groups in the country, and stability was maintained only by harsh repression by both Hafiz and Bashar Assad. Little sense of loyalty to an entity called Syria transcended loyalties to one's sect, ethnic group, or religion, and when the repressive state looked as if it was weakening, as in 2011, the country fell apart.

Weak national identity has been a major problem in the greater Middle East, where Yemen and Libya have turned into failed states, and Afghanistan, Iraq, and Somalia have suffered from internal insurgency and chaos. Other developing countries have remained more stable, yet remain beset by problems related to a weak sense of national identity. This is the situation throughout sub-Saharan Africa, and it is a major obstacle to development. Countries such as Kenya and Nigeria, for example, are ethnically and religiously divided; stability is maintained only because different ethnic groups take turns in power to loot the country.[1] High levels of corruption, poverty, and failed economic development are the result.

By contrast, Japan, Korea, and China all had well-developed national identities well before they began to modernize—indeed, prior to their confrontation with the Western powers in the nineteenth century. Part of the reason they have been able to grow in such spectacular fashion in the twentieth and early twenty-first centuries is that they did not have to settle internal questions of identity as they opened up to international trade and investment. They too suffered from civil war, occupation, and division. But they could build on traditions of statehood and common national purpose once these conflicts were stabilized.

National identity begins with a shared belief in the legitimacy of the country's political system, whether that system is democratic or not. Identity can be embodied in formal laws and institutions that dictate, for example, what the educational system will teach children about their country's past, or what will be considered an official national language. But national identity also extends into the realm of culture and values. It consists of the stories that people tell about themselves: where they came from, what they celebrate, their shared historical memories, what it takes to become a genuine member of the community.[2]

In the contemporary world, diversity—on the basis of race, ethnicity, religion, gender, sexual orientation, and the like—is both a fact of life and a value. For many reasons it is a good thing for societies. Exposure to different ways of thinking and acting can often stimulate innovation, creativity, and entrepreneurship. Diversity provides interest and excitement. In the year 1970, Washington, D.C., was a rather boring biracial city in which the most exotic food one would dine on was served at the Yenching Palace on Connecticut Avenue. Today, the greater Washington area is home to an incredible amount of ethnic diversity: one can get Ethiopian, Peruvian, Cambodian, and Pakistani food and travel from one small ethnic enclave to another. The internationalization of the city has stimulated other forms of interest: as it becomes a place where young people want to live, they bring new music, arts, technologies, and entire neighborhoods that didn't exist before. Washington's story has been replicated in any number of other metropolitan areas around the world, from Chicago to San Francisco to London to Berlin.

Diversity is also critical to resilience. Environmental biologists point out that artificially produced crop monocultures are often highly vulnerable to diseases because the population lacks genetic diversity. Indeed, genetic diversity is the motor of evolution itself, which is based on genetic variation and adaptation. The broad concern over the loss of diversity in species around the world rests on its threat to long-term biological resilience.

Finally, there is the matter of the individual search for identity that we have examined in earlier chapters. People often resist being homogenized into larger cultures, particularly if they were not born into them. They want their specific selves to be recognized and celebrated, not suppressed. They want to feel a connection with their ancestors and know where they came from. Even if they are not part of the culture, they want to hold on to the world's fast-disappearing indigenous languages, and traditional practices that recall earlier ways of life.

On the other hand, diversity is not an unalloyed good. Syria and Afghanistan are very diverse places, but such diversity yields violence and conflict rather than creativity and resilience. Kenya's diversity sharpens the divisions between ethnic groups and feeds an inward-looking political corruption. Ethnic diversity led to the breakdown of the liberal Austro-Hungarian Empire in the decades prior to World War I, when its component nationalities decided they could not live together in a common political structure. Fin de siècle Vienna was a melting pot that had produced Gustav Mahler, Hugo von Hofmannsthal, and Sigmund Freud. But when the empire's narrower national identities—Serbs, Bulgarians, Czechs, and Austro-Germans—asserted themselves, the region descended into a paroxysm of violence and intolerance.[3]

National identity got a bad name in this period precisely because it came to be associated with an exclusive, ethnically based sense of belonging known as ethno-nationalism. This type of identity persecuted people who were not part of the group and committed aggressions against foreigners on behalf of co-ethnics living in other countries. The problem, however, was not with the idea of national identity itself; the problem was the narrow, ethnically based, intolerant, aggressive, and deeply illiberal form that national identity took.

Things do not have to be this way. National identities can be built around liberal and democratic political values, and the common experiences that provide the connective tissue around which diverse communities can thrive. India, France, Canada, and the United States are examples of countries that have tried to do this. Such an inclusive sense of national identity remains critical for the maintenance of a successful modern political order for a number of reasons.

The first is physical security. The extreme example of what can happen absent national identity is state breakdown and civil war, as in such cases as Syria or Libya, noted above. But short of this, weak national identity creates other serious security issues. Large political units are more powerful than smaller ones and can protect themselves better. They are in a better position to shape the international environment to suit their own interests. Britain, for example, could not have played nearly the same role on the geopolitical stage as it has in the past centuries if Scotland had remained an independent country. The same would be true for Spain if its richest region, Catalonia, seceded. Highly divided countries are weak, which is why Putin's Russia has provided quiet support to independence movements across Europe and has intervened in American politics to increase the level of political division there.[4]

Second, national identity is important for the quality of government. Good government—that is, effective public services and low levels of corruption—depends on state officials placing public interest above their own narrow interests. In systemically corrupt societies, politicians and bureaucrats divert public resources to their own ethnic group, region, tribe, family, political party, or to their own individual pockets because they do not feel obligated to the community's general interests.

This points to a third function of national identity: facilitating economic development. If people do not take pride in their country, they will not work on its behalf. The strong national identities in Japan, South Korea, and China produced elites that were intensely focused on their countries' economic development rather than on their personal enrichment, particularly during the early decades of rapid economic growth. This kind of public-directedness underlay the "developmental state" and was much less common in such regions as sub-Saharan Africa, the Middle East, or Latin America.[5] Many identity groups based on ethnicity or religion prefer to trade among themselves and use their access to state power to benefit their group alone.

While this may be of help to an immigrant community newly arrived in a country, their future prosperity will depend critically on their ability to assimilate into the larger culture. Economies thrive on having access to the widest possible markets, where transactions will be completed without regard to the identities of the buyers and sellers—provided, of course, that national identity does not become the basis for protectionism against other nations.[6]

A fourth function of national identity is to promote a wide radius of trust. Trust acts like a lubricant that facilitates both economic exchange and political participation. Trust is based on what has been called social capital, that is, the ability to cooperate with other people based on informal norms and shared values. Identity groups promote trust among their members, but social capital often remains limited to the narrow in-group. Indeed, strong identities often *decrease* trust between in- and out-group members. Societies thrive on trust, but they need the widest possible radius of trust to do well.[7]

A fifth reason national identity is important is to maintain strong social safety nets that mitigate economic inequality. If members of a society feel that they are members of an extended family and have high levels of trust in one another, they are much more likely to support social programs that aid their weaker fellows. The strong welfare states of Scandinavia are underpinned by their equally strong senses of national identity. By contrast, societies divided into self-regarding social groups who feel they have little in common are more likely to regard themselves as in a zero-sum competition with one another for resources.[8]

The final function of national identity is to make possible liberal democracy itself. A liberal democracy is an implicit contract between citizens and their government, and among the citizens themselves, under which they give up certain rights in order that the government protects other rights that are more basic and important. National identity is built around the legitimacy of this contract; if citizens do not believe they are part of the same polity, the system will not function.[9]

But the quality of democracy depends on more than mere acceptance of the system's basic rules. Democracies need their own culture to function. They do not produce automatic agreement; indeed, they are necessarily pluralistic collections of diverse interests, opinions, and values that have to be reconciled peacefully. Democracies require deliberation and debate, which can happen only if people accept certain norms of behavior on what can be said and done. Citizens often have to accept outcomes they do not like or prefer, in the interest of a common good; a culture of tolerance and mutual sympathy must override partisan passions.

Identity is rooted in thymos, which is experienced emotionally through feelings of pride, shame, and anger. I've already noted the ways in which this can undermine rational debate and deliberation. On the other hand, democracies will not survive if citizens are not in some measure irrationally attached to the ideas of constitutional government and human equality through feelings of pride and patriotism. These attachments will see societies through their low points, when reason alone may counsel despair at the working of institutions.

The policy issue that has raised the greatest challenges to national identity is immigration, and the related issue of refugees. Together, they are the driving force behind the upsurge of populist nationalism in both Europe and the United States. France's National Front, the Freedom Party in the Netherlands, Viktor Orbán's Fidesz in Hungary, the AfD in Germany, and the Brexiteers in the United Kingdom are both anti-immigrant and opposed to the European Union. But for many populists, these are the same issue: they intensely dislike the EU because they think it is depriving them of their sovereign right to control their own borders. The EU had created the Schengen system of visa-free travel within most of its member states in 1985, in the interests of labor mobility and economic growth. In addition, the EU has granted extensive rights to refugees once they enter Europe, rights that are enforced not by national courts but by the European Court of Human Rights.*

This system has worked as advertised, allowing labor to flow to areas where it can be used more productively, and offering refuge to victims of political persecution. But it has also led to massive increases in the numbers of foreign-born individuals in many EU countries, an issue that came to a head in 2014 when the Syrian civil war sent more than a million Syrians into Europe.

Similarly, in the United States, immigration has largely displaced class and race as the chief reason why Americans vote for Republican candidates, according to data by political scientists Zoltan Hajnal and Marisa Abrajano.[10] The incorporation of African-Americans into the Democratic Party following the civil rights movement of the 1960s is widely credited for driving the South into the arms of the Republican Party; today immigration is playing a similar role. Opposition to Mexican and Muslim immigration figured centrally in Donald Trump's election campaign and subsequent rise to the presidency. At the core of conservative complaints over immigration are the

---

* The Schengen zone overlaps with but does not completely correspond to either the EU or the eurozone; some EU countries such as Ireland and the United Kingdom opted out, while non-EU states such as Iceland and Norway are de facto parts of the zone.

approximately 11–12 million undocumented immigrants now estimated to be living in the United States. As in Europe, anti-immigrant politicians bemoan the country's failure to exercise its sovereign right to control the flow of people across its southern borders. Hence Trump's promise of a "big, beautiful" wall on the Mexican border.

It should not be surprising that immigration has triggered a backlash, since levels of migrants and corresponding cultural change have been high and in some cases historically unprecedented. Table 2 provides data on the numbers of foreign-born individuals in a group of rich countries over the past sixty years. Levels in the United States are today as high as they were in the 1920s following the large wave of immigrants who entered the country before and after the turn of the twentieth century.

The common objective of populist politicians in both Europe and the United States is to "take back our country." They argue that traditional understandings of national identity are being diluted and overtaken both by newcomers with different values and cultures and by a progressive left that attacks the very idea of national identity as racist and intolerant.

But what country are they trying to take back? The U.S. Constitution begins with the statement "We, the People of the United States, in Order to form a more perfect Union, establish Justice, insure domestic Tranquility, provide for the common defence, promote the general Welfare, and secure the Blessings of Liberty to ourselves and our Posterity, do ordain and establish this Constitution for the United States of America." The Constitution says clearly that the people are sovereign and that legitimate government flows from their will. But it does not define who the people are, or on what basis individuals are to be included in the national community.

TABLE 2

Foreign-Born as Percentage of Population, Selected Organisation for Economic Co-operation and Development (OECD) Countries

	1960	1970	1980	1990	2000	2013	2015	2016
Australia	...	...	...	22.769	23.037	27.713	...	...
Austria	10.57	9.06	9.54	10.33	10.395	16.704	18.2	...
Belgium	...	...	...	...	10.328	15.508	16.3	...
Canada	...	...	...	15.234	17.36	19.993	...	...
Denmark	...	...	...	3.689	5.781	8.478	...	...
Finland	...	0.705	0.811	1.27	2.631	5.594	6	...
France	7.49	8.31	10.64	10.4	10.13	12.04	...	...
Germany	...	...	...	...	12.402	12.776	13.3	...
Greece	6.3	10.19	1.798	6.06	10.28	...	...	12.7
Hungary	...	3.89	3.45	3.35	2.885	4.525	5.1	...
Ireland	2.58	4.41	6.54	6.49	8.665	16.42	16.9	...

Italy	0.915	1.6	1.97	2.52	3.73	9.457	9.7
Japan	0.56	0.587	0.65	0.871	1.02	...	1.4
Korea	0.316	0.42	1.23	0.1	0.321	...	2.6
Netherlands	...	2	3.47	8.14	10.143	11.625	12.1
New Zealand	14.08	14.57	15.11	15.56	17.187	22.406	...
Norway	...	...	...	...	6.792	13.868	14.9
Poland	...	...	...	7.75	5.6	...	1.6
Spain	0.696	0.95	1.31	2.12	4.891	13.439	12.7
Sweden	...	6.55	7.52	9.22	11.314	15.973	17
Switzerland	...	13.41	16.87	20.73	21.864	28.303	27.9
United Kingdom	...	5.29	5.96	...	7.925	12.261	13.3
United States	...	...	...	7.919	11.024	13.079	13.44

Source: OECD.

This silence in the American Constitution raises some important questions: Where does national identity come from in the first place, and how is it defined? What makes for a "people," whose sovereignty is the basis for democratic choice? Is multiculturalism, both de facto and as an ideology, weakening our sense of common citizenship, and if so, are there means of rebuilding a shared understanding of national identity across populations that are diverse?

The American Constitution's failure to define who the American people are reflects a broader problem for all liberal democracies. The political theorist Pierre Manent notes that most democracies were built on top of preexisting nations, societies that already had a well-developed sense of national identity that defined the sovereign people. But those nations were not created democratically: Germany, France, Britain, and the Netherlands were all the historical by-products of long and often violent political struggles over territory and culture under nondemocratic regimes. When these societies democratized, their territorial extent and their existing populations were simply taken for granted as the basis for popular sovereignty. A similar story could be told for Japan and Korea in East Asia, which were nations centuries before they democratized and did not have to litigate issues of peoplehood as they opened up politics to democratic choice.[11]

Manent identifies a major gap in modern democratic theory. Thinkers such as Thomas Hobbes, John Locke, Jean-Jacques Rousseau, Immanuel Kant, the authors of the Federalist Papers, and John Stuart Mill all assumed that the world was predivided into nations that formed the foundation of democratic choice. They did not provide a theory of why the border between the United States and Mexico should run along the Rio Grande, whether Alsace should belong to France or Germany, whether Quebec should be part of Canada or a "distinct society," on what grounds Catalonia could legitimately separate itself from Spain, or what the proper level of immigration should be.

Such theorizing has been left to others. Nationalists such as Paul de Lagarde or Adolf Hitler grounded their definitions of nation in biology and argued that the existing nations of the world constituted racial entities that had existed from time immemorial. Others made an allegedly unchanging inherited culture the basis for nationhood. Such theories became the justification for the aggressive nationalisms of early twentieth-century Europe, whose exponents were defeated with the fall of Nazism in 1945.

Those one might characterize as "global cosmopolitans" argue that the very concepts of national identity and state sovereignty are outmoded and need to be replaced by broader transnational identities and institutions. Two types of argument underpin this school. The first is economic and functional, saying that problems today are global in scope and therefore need to be addressed globally. Such issues range from trade and investment to counterterrorism, the environment, infectious diseases, narcotics, human trafficking, and many others. Nations and national identities are potential obstacles to international cooperation and need to be gradually superseded by a new layer of transnational rules and organizations.

The second strand of argument is more theoretical and comes out of international human rights law. Liberal democracies are built on a premise of universal human equality, and that equality does not begin or end at national borders. The 1948 Universal Declaration of Human Rights became the basis for a growing body of international law that asserted that rights are inherent in all human beings and need to be respected by all nations.[12] As human rights law has evolved, so have the obligations of states not just to their own citizens, but to immigrants and refugees as well. Some advocates have even posited a universal right to migrate.[13]

Both of these arguments are valid to some degree. But they do not undermine the case for an international order built around national states, or for the necessity of the right sort of national identity within those states. The idea that states are obsolete and should be superseded by international bodies is flawed because no one has been able to come up with a good method for holding such international bodies democratically accountable. The functioning of democratic institutions depends on shared norms, perspectives, and ultimately culture, all of which can exist on the level of a national state, but which do not exist internationally. Effective international cooperation can and has been built instead around cooperation between existing states. For decades now nations have been giving up aspects of their sovereignty to protect their national interests.[14] The kinds of cooperative agreements needed to resolve a host of issues can continue to be addressed in this fashion.

The obligation to respect universal human rights has been voluntarily undertaken by most countries around the world, and rightly so. But all liberal democracies are built on top of states, whose jurisdiction is limited by their territorial reach. No state can undertake an unlimited obligation to protect people outside its jurisdiction, and whether the world would be better off if they all tried to do so is not clear. While countries rightly feel a moral obligation to shelter refugees and may welcome immigrants, such obligations are potentially costly both economically and socially, and democracies need to balance them against other priorities. Democracy means that the people are sovereign, but if there is no way of delimiting who the people are, they cannot exercise democratic choice.

Thus political order both at home and internationally will depend on the continuing existence of liberal democracies with the right kind of inclusive national identities. But we have yet to explain the provenance of such identities in existing democracies, and how they might change in the future.

13

STORIES OF PEOPLEHOOD

It is difficult to theorize about national identity because existing nations are the by-product of complex and messy historical
struggles that have often been violent and coercive. The result-
ing nations are workable platforms on which to create democratic institutions, but the outcomes continue to be contested
and are constantly challenged by demographic, economic, and
political change.

National identities have been created by four main paths.
The first is to transfer populations across the political boundaries of a particular country, either by sending settlers into
new territories, by forcibly evicting people who live in a certain
territory, or by simply killing them off—or all three. The third
of these was labeled ethnic cleansing during the Balkan wars
of the early 1990s and was rightly condemned by the international community. But ethnic cleansing has been used by many
countries in the past, including democracies such as Australia,
New Zealand, Chile, and the United States, which saw settlers

violently removing or killing off the indigenous populations of the territories in which they settled.

The second path to nationhood is to move borders to fit existing linguistic or cultural populations. Historically, this has been accomplished either through unification, as in the case of Italy and Germany in the 1860s and '70s, or through separation, as when the Irish Republic left the United Kingdom in 1919, or when Ukraine declared its independence from the former Soviet Union in 1991.

The third path is to assimilate minority populations into the culture of an existing ethnic or linguistic group. France was a polyglot nation two hundred years ago, but over time the different local languages such as Provençal, Breton, or Flemish were gradually displaced by Parisian French. Similarly, immigrants to Argentina or the United States—or more likely, their children—learned Spanish or English to fit into the dominant culture and move up the social ladder. The apparent ethnic homogeneity of China, where more than 90 percent of the population are said to be Han Chinese, was the product of a lengthy cultural and biological assimilation of minority populations over three millennia.

The fourth path is to reshape national identity to fit the existing characteristics of the society in question. Contrary to the views of many nationalists, "nations" are not biological entities that have existed from time immemorial; they are socially constructed from the bottom up and the top down. Those doing the constructing can deliberately shape identities to suit people's characteristics and habits. An example were India's founders Gandhi and Nehru, who built on an existing "idea of India" that would incorporate that society's extremely diverse population.[1] The founders of Indonesia and Tanzania in effect created new national languages to unify their highly diverse societies.[2]

The policies that do the most to shape national identity are rules regarding citizenship and residency, laws on immigration and refugees, and the curricula used in the public education system to teach children about the nation's past. As well, in a bottom-up process, "stories of peoplehood" are told by a society's artists, musicians, poets, filmmakers, historians, and ordinary citizens who describe their own provenance and aspirations.

One of the most vivid illustrations of how nation building takes place in a democratic society was portrayed in the film *Invictus*, which tells the story of South Africa's hosting of the Rugby World Cup in 1995. The new democratic South Africa that emerged from apartheid in the early 1990s was sharply fragmented along racial and ethnic lines. One of the cleavages was in sports, where whites followed rugby and blacks played soccer. The country's visionary first president, Nelson Mandela, understood the importance of sports to national self-consciousness and deliberately sought to build support for the mostly white national rugby team, the Springboks, among the country's black population. He did this against the opposition of his own African National Congress. He could not impose this preference on his followers; he had to cajole and persuade them. It helped that the Springboks eventually won the rugby title. They did this by beating New Zealand's powerful All Blacks, a team that employs a bit of nation building itself when it performs a Maori war dance, the haka, before every game.

All four of the paths to national identity can be accomplished peacefully and consensually, or through violence and coercion. All existing nations are the historical by-product of some combination of the four and drew on some combination of coercion and consensus. The challenge facing contemporary liberal democracies in the face of immigration and growing diversity is to undertake some combination of the third and fourth paths—to define an inclusive national identity that fits the society's diverse reality, and to assimilate newcomers to that identity. What is at stake in this task is the preservation of liberal democracy itself.

The contemporary European struggle over national identity begins with the founders of the European Union, Robert Schuman and Jean Monnet, who understood that exclusive ethnic definitions of national identity had been at the root of the two world wars that Europe experienced.[3] As an antidote, they created the European Coal and Steel Community in 1951, composed of France, Belgium, West Germany, Italy, the Netherlands, and Luxembourg, which was designed to prevent German rearmament while facilitating trade and economic cooperation in a formerly integrated region that had been ripped apart by war. The Coal and Steel Community evolved in stages into the European Economic Community and eventually into the EU, with a membership that grew steadily to encompass the current twenty-eight members.

The founders of the European Union deliberately sought to weaken national identities at the member-state level in favor of a "postnational" European consciousness, as an antidote to the aggressive ethno-nationalisms of the first half of the twentieth century.[4] The hope of these founders was that economic interdependence would make war less likely, and that political cooperation would follow on its heels. In many ways, they were wildly successful: the idea that Germany and France, the two main antagonists of the world wars, would ever go to war with each other is vanishingly remote today. A stratum of young, usually well-educated Europeans are now born in one member state, get their education in another, marry someone from yet another country, and work in multiple locations within the EU and farther afield. They retain an awareness of their birth nationality, but their lives are tied to the EU as a whole.

But whether "Europe" has an identity stronger than the old national identities it was supposed to supersede is not clear. In the EU's early decades, it was not politically acceptable to celebrate national identity too loudly at a member-state level. This was particularly true for countries such as Germany and Spain that had fascist pasts: citizens did not wave national flags, sing national anthems, or cheer too loudly for their country's sports teams. For them Europe was a refuge, but not necessarily a preferred destination.

But the leaders of the EU were not in a position to invest much effort in building an alternative new identity.[5] They did not create a single European citizenship; rules for citizenship remained the province of individual member states. The symbols of nationhood such as a flag and an anthem came late, and the EU's diverse membership had no common civic education. But the most important failure was in the democratic accountability of the EU itself. The most powerful institution within the EU was the European Commission, an unelected technocratic body whose main purpose was to promote a single market within Europe. It was answerable to the people only indirectly, via the Council of Ministers, which represented the individual member states. A directly elected European parliament had rather limited powers, which has consequently failed to generate significant voter turnout or enthusiasm. Citizens of Europe knew that the important votes they cast were still those at the member-state level, and their chief energies and emotional attachments were directed there. As a result, they felt little sense of ownership or control over the institutions governing Europe as a whole.

So while the elites talked of "ever-closer union" within the EU, the reality was that the ghosts of the older national identities hung around like unwanted guests at a dinner party. This was particularly true among older, less educated voters who could not or would not take advantage of the mobility offered by the new Europe. These ghosts started to emerge at critical junctures, where they have created an existential threat to the EU as a whole.

This was vividly illustrated by the crisis over the euro, in which the common currency, issued first in 1999, allowed Greece to borrow profligately during the boom years of the 2000s. The Germans, who were perfectly willing to support their less well-off fellow citizens with an expansive welfare state, were not inclined to be so generous with the Greeks when the latter threatened to default. Greece indeed had very different approaches to savings, debt, and practices such as public-sector patronage than did Germany. Berlin, as Greece's chief creditor, was able to impose crushing austerity on Athens with help from international institutions such as the European Central Bank and the IMF, a situation that persists to the present. The euro crisis exposed a deep rift within the eurozone's northern and southern members, who today are far more aware of their national differences than they were prior to the outbreak of the crisis.

But the more significant conflict emerged over the related questions of immigration and refugees. Levels of foreign-born residents began to rise dramatically in the 1990s and 2000s for a number of reasons. First, the guest workers from Muslim-majority countries such as Turkey, Pakistan, and Morocco did not return home as initially expected; rather, they brought their families, had children, and started to settle in to their adopted countries. The dramatic expansion of the EU following the end of the Cold War opened the gates to massive immigration from Eastern Europe to the west, just as economic theory suggested it might as workers sought job opportunities in richer countries.

Migration from Muslim countries was always more controversial in Europe than was migration from elsewhere in the EU. The reasons for this were complex. In some cases, it was the result of simple racism, xenophobia, and cultural prejudice. Others feared that the newcomers were not "fitting into" the host societies. Charges were made that immigrants and their children were living in self-enclosed neighborhoods and not learning the national language even after years of residence.

These fears became far more vivid after the September 11 attacks on the World Trade Center in New York, followed quickly by a string of similar al-Qaeda operations in London and Madrid. These incidents triggered bitter debates over national identity in many European countries, since the terrorists often came from within their own societies. This was particularly the case in the Netherlands, which has, proportionately, one of Europe's highest levels of Muslim immigrants. The controversy was started when Pim Fortuyn, an openly gay politician, argued in favor of closing off Muslim immigration on the grounds that Muslims were intolerant of people such as himself and would not fit into Holland's permissive culture. Fortuyn was assassinated outside a radio station in May 2002, not by a Muslim but by an animal rights activist. But in 2004, Theo van Gogh, a Dutch filmmaker, was murdered by Mohammed Bouyeri, a Dutch citizen of Moroccan extraction who was enraged by one of van Gogh's films that the killer felt was disrespectful of Islam.

A further wave of violence occurred in Europe following the establishment of the Islamic State in Syria and Iraq in the wake of the Syrian civil war. These included the *Charlie Hebdo* incident in Paris in January 2015, the Bataclan attacks later that year that led to 130 deaths, the bombing of the Brussels airport in March 2016, and attacks making use of trucks to mow down pedestrians in Berlin, London, Nice, and New York City. A significant group of Muslims had been radicalized by the Syrian conflict, and by recruitment over the internet by radical preachers.

These attacks focused attention on citizenship and national identity precisely because so many of the attackers were citizens of the countries they attacked and second-generation children of immigrants. Many European countries, it became clear, were harboring growing populations of angry immigrants who were not being properly integrated into their host societies, a small number of whom indeed seemed to bear deep hatred for the values those societies espoused.

Earlier challenges to national identity did not seem so serious. Multiculturalism was born in some sense in Canada, where the French-speaking population in Quebec wanted the legal right to protect their language and education in a continent dominated by English speakers. The Meech Lake Accord, negotiated in 1987, would have amended Canada's constitution to protect the province as a "distinct society." It was controversial precisely because it constituted a form of unequal group recognition: French Canadians were to be given linguistic rights not enjoyed by English speakers. The accord was not approved, but Canadian federalism continues to protect Quebec's special cultural rights by mandating the use of French by French speakers and immigrants.

Muslim immigrants tested the limits of multiculturalism in ways that the Quebec nationalists did not. The latter's most extreme demands would have split Canada into two countries, but even a separation would not have represented a fundamental threat to democratic values, since an independent Quebec would have remained a high-quality liberal democratic state. The real impact of francophone cultural demands concerns Canada's linguistic rules, which were at most an annoyance to English speakers who had to learn French and post bilingual signs.

The same was not necessarily true of some of the cultural beliefs and practices of Muslim communities. The most extreme cases were Muslims willing to commit terrorism against their fellow citizens. Overt violence crossed a clear threshold and would be intolerable in any society. Other practices were more complex. Many Muslim families arranged the marriages of their daughters, potentially contravening the rights of the young women to choose their own partners; some unlucky ones who disobeyed became the targets of honor killings. Many observant Muslims disapproved of homosexuality at a time when gay marriage was spreading like wildfire across Europe. Muslim groups, in the name of respect for culture, made demands to be treated differently: to be allowed to segregate women and girls, or to prohibit women from being treated by male doctors and nurses. And as a result of the bitter Israeli-Palestinian conflict, many Muslims displayed a kind of anti-Semitism that Europe had been vigilant in suppressing since the end of World War II.

The 2000s saw the emergence of an intense debate across Europe over citizenship, immigration, and national identity. Citizenship is a two-way street: it endows citizens with rights that are protected by the state, but it also enjoins duties on them, above all, the duty of loyalty to the country's principles and laws. This was a particularly neuralgic issue due to the large welfare benefits of many European states: strong opposition arose to providing such benefits to immigrants who did not seem to accept the basic terms of the social contract. And some feared that Muslims, as opposed to earlier immigrant groups, might never properly assimilate into the countries' cultures. Right-wing anti-immigrant parties such as the National Front in France, Denmark's Danish People's Party, and the Freedom Party in the Netherlands gained support and put pressure on mainstream parties to accommodate their demands.

As a result, many European countries began to rethink their citizenship laws, and therefore the grounds on which immigrants could become full members of their societies. The failure to assimilate immigrants was not a one-way street: many European democracies made citizenship hard to obtain. Citizenship can be granted at birth on the basis of jus soli or jus sanguinis, or it can be acquired after birth through naturalization. Under jus soli, anyone born on the country's territory automatically became a citizen; under jus sanguinis, citizenship depends on descent.[6] The United States has always had a jus soli, but it was actualized for people of all races with passage of the Fourteenth Amendment in 1868, which states, "All persons born or naturalized in the United States, and subject to the jurisdiction thereof, are citizens of the United States and of the state wherein they reside." Similar rules apply in countries such as Australia and Canada with relatively open attitudes toward immigration.[7]

In Europe, the French have a long history of thinking of citizenship in political and territorial terms; though technically practicing jus sanguinis, their relatively easy terms for naturalization have permitted the almost-automatic acquisition of citizenship for second- and third-generation immigrants.[8] French nationality has traditionally been defined as loyalty to the republic, the French language, and a French education; the Senegalese poet Léopold Senghor was admitted to the prestigious Académie Française in 1983 because of his contributions to French literature.

Germany, Austria, and Switzerland (as well as Asian democracies such as Japan and South Korea) have by contrast traditionally based citizenship on jus sanguinis and have made naturalization difficult. Before Germany's laws were somewhat liberalized in 2000, second- and third-generation children of immigrant parents from Turkey or other Middle Eastern countries speaking perfect German could obtain citizenship only with great difficulty. By contrast, ethnic Germans from the former Soviet Union and other Eastern Bloc countries could be naturalized on proof of German ethnicity, even if they spoke no German.[9] Japan has one of the most restrictive systems of citizenship and naturalization of any developed democracy, as well as sharp limits on immigration, with the result that it is one of the least diverse of the Organisation for Economic Co-operation and Development (OECD) countries.[10]

Individual European countries began reforming their citizenship laws in the 2000s.[11] In some respects these changes were helpful to social integration, shifting away from jus sanguinis and establishing a set of criteria for naturalization that could be plausibly met by an aspiring immigrant. New citizens were expected to demonstrate knowledge of the country's history, to understand its political institutions, and to speak the national language with a certain proficiency. But in some cases, these requirements were made so demanding that it seemed they were meant to exclude rather than include. The German state of Baden-Württemberg, for example, made acceptance of gay marriage a condition of citizenship, a curious requirement in light of its own conservative Catholic heritage.[12]

Beyond these formal citizenship rules, outright racism and

other, more subtle cultural barriers deterred assimilation.[13] Adjectives such as *German, Dutch*, and *Danish* have always had an ethnic connotation. Whereas an immigrant to the United States born in Guatemala or Korea can proudly assert that he or she is an American from the moment after taking the naturalization oath, it is much harder for German citizens of Turkish descent to say that they are German, even if they were born in the country and speak German as their native language. The Netherlands is famously tolerant, but that tolerance is built around parallel communities rather than integration on an individual level. Under "pillarization" (*verzuiling*), the Protestant, Catholic, and secular communities for many years maintained their own schools, newspapers, and political parties. When Muslims started arriving in significant numbers, they were often channeled into their own pillar, where they attended school only with other Muslim children. The Dutch system had worked well historically in maintaining social peace in a divided society, but in the twenty-first century it is an obstacle to assimilating immigrants of a very different culture.

The new Eastern European member states of the European Union were even less willing to accept culturally different newcomers than the original founding countries. The Soviet occupation of the region after 1945 and its imposition of Communism on them froze their social and political development. Unlike West Germany or Spain, they were not forced to wrestle with their nationalist pasts, nor did they make an effort to entrench liberal values in their citizens. They had virtually no experience with immigration and were among the least diverse societies in the developed world. After 1989 they gladly threw off Communism and rushed into the EU, but many of their citizens did not embrace the positive liberal values embodied in the new Europe. As a result, Hungary's Viktor Orbán could declare that Hungarian national identity was based on Hungarian ethnicity, just as Adolf Hitler had declared that German identity was based on German blood. Brussels was seen by many new Eastern European leaders as a threat, primarily because it opened the door to unlimited immigration from the Middle East and Africa.

Another EU member state that had never fully accepted a European identity was Britain. For years Britain was the one key EU country that possessed a loud Euroskeptic fringe, represented by important parts of the Conservative Party and by newer groups such as the UK Independence Party (UKIP) under Nigel Farage.[14] Britain's unexpected vote to leave the European Union in June 2016 was predicted to have disastrous economic consequences, but the issue for many Leave voters was one of identity rather than economics. The vote is perhaps understandable in light of the historical legacy of English identity.

English Euroskepticism is rooted in a long-standing belief in English exceptionalism. The country was conquered in 1066 by a French dynasty and for the next several hundred years had a history deeply intertwined with that of the Continent. But when Henry VIII broke with the papacy in the early sixteenth century and created a separate Protestant national church, a distinctive sense of English identity began to take root. According to the historian Alan Smith,

> the feeling of national identity and uniqueness continued to grow, reaching an apogee in the reign of Elizabeth when it was given classic expression in one of the most influential works in the whole of English literature. John Foxe's *Acts and Monuments* . . . was a resounding statement of the theory that Protestant England was God's "elect nation," superior to the enslaved Papists of the Continent and entirely independent of

all authority apart from that of the Crown . . . That was the theory of English and later of British nationhood which was to prevail from then onwards until the 1970s, when membership of the European Community once more subjected the country to the decisions of an external authority.[15]

This sense of separation was strengthened by the country's defeat of the Spanish Armada, and by the political struggles surrounding the Civil War in the seventeenth century, which established the sovereignty of Parliament. That hard-won sovereignty was something not easily given up: if one listens to the rhetoric of the Brexiteers, the Continent is still enslaved, this time not by a pope or emperor, but by the European Union.

National identity in Europe is today confused, to put it charitably. Proponents of the European Union have not succeeded in creating a strong sense of pan-European identity that supersedes the identities of its member states. Those national identities are tenacious and vary tremendously among themselves, ranging from relatively open ones that could accommodate diverse populations, like that of France, to others that create deliberate barriers to the assimilation of immigrants, such as the one espoused by Hungary. The region is not threatened by immigrants so much as by the political reaction that immigrants and cultural diversity create. The anti-immigrant, anti-EU demons that have been summoned are often deeply illiberal and could undermine the open political order on which the region's prosperity has been based. Dealing with this backlash will depend not on a rejection of identity itself, but on the deliberate shaping of national identities in ways that promote a sense of democratic and open community.

Compared to most European countries, the United States has had a longer experience with immigration and has developed a national identity better suited to assimilating newcomers. But this identity was the product of political struggles over prolonged periods and even today is not settled. It has been sharply contested by some since the election of Donald Trump as president in 2016.

Trump built his campaign around opposition to immigration, especially from Mexico and the Muslim world. Like their anti-immigrant counterparts in Europe, many of Trump's supporters assert they want to "take back their country," a claim that implies their country has somehow been stolen from them. An August 2017 "Unite the Right" rally in Charlottesville, Virginia, brought together neo-Nazi and racist groups chanting "blood and soil," and a torchlight rally deliberately reminiscent of National Socialism. In response to the rally, Republican senator Ben Sasse tweeted, "These people are utterly revolting—and have no understanding of America. This creedal nation explicitly rejects 'blood and soil' nationalism."[16]

Sasse's sentiment that the United States is a creedal nation was highly laudable, especially in the face of a president who seemed to sympathize with many of the ugly sentiments on display at the rally, and the rank cowardice by other Republican politicians who failed to criticize him. But American national identity has evolved over the years; a creedal identity has emerged after decades of political struggle and is to this day not accepted by all Americans.

In Federalist No. 2, John Jay opens the debate on the proposed American Constitution in the following terms:

> Providence has been pleased to give this one connected country to one united people—a people descended from the same ancestors, speaking the same language, professing the

same religion, attached to the same principles of government, very similar in their manner and customs, and who, by their joint counsels, arms, and efforts, fighting side by side through a long and bloody war, have nobly established general liberty and independence.

Note how specific and narrow Jay's definition of American identity is. It is based on shared religion (Protestantism), ethnicity (descent from the English), common language (English), and belief in the same republican principles of government. Even Thomas Paine, considered a left-wing radical at the time of the Revolution, claimed brotherhood only with "every European Christian." Thomas Jefferson doubted that he shared the same blood as the "Scotch" and worried about immigrants from the wrong parts of Europe coming to the United States, who would bring "the principles of the government they leave, imbibed in their early youth; or, if able to throw them off, it will be in exchange for an unbounded licentiousness."[17]

Jefferson was not the only historical figure worried that the American character would be corrupted by importing the wrong type of person. The arrival of large numbers of Irish Catholics in the 1840s triggered a nativist reaction fearful of the effects of "Popery" and alcoholism, a fear that eventually played out in the passage of the Eighteenth Amendment on Prohibition in 1917. The country's Anglo-Saxon Protestant elites at times feared German immigrants, who might bring their absolutist instincts to the United States. This fear peaked after the country's entry into World War I, when many German Americans sought to hide their ethnic heritage. The same was true for the millions of Southern and Eastern Europeans who arrived in the great immigration wave that began in the 1880s and lasted until passage of the Johnson-Reed Act in 1924, which limited entry to the United States by national origin.

Religion and ethnicity were, in other words, key components of the way that many Americans thought about themselves. But a creedal narrative as well had equally deep historical roots, a narrative that contested this view. The French immigrant Hector St. John Crèvecoeur wrote in the 1780s that America was "the asylum of freedom, as the cradle of future nations, and the refuge of distressed Europeans" where "all sects are mixed as well as all nations." George Washington portrayed a political understanding of the soon-to-be United States as a place "open to receive not only the Opulent and respectable Stranger, but the oppressed and persecuted of all Nations and Religions." The same Thomas Paine who could only imagine brotherhood with other Christians elsewhere saw the United States as made up "of people from different nations, speaking different languages," but for whom "by the simple operation of constructing government on the principles of society and the Rights of Man, every difficulty retires and all the parts are brought into cordial unison."[18] These sentiments underlie the mottoes adorning the Great Seal of the United States: *Novus ordo seclorum* ("New order of the ages") and *E pluribus unum* ("From many, one").

The American Civil War was, at its root, a fight over American national identity. The Southern states explicitly linked identity to race by excluding nonwhites from citizenship. They drew on the founding principles of the Constitution to argue, as Stephen Douglas did, that democratic majorities in each state had the right to vote slavery up or down as they wished, and that the federal government had no right to interfere in this choice. Abraham Lincoln, by contrast, appealed not to the Constitution but to the Declaration of Independence, and the latter's assertion that "all men are created equal." In his debates with Douglas, Lincoln argued that this principle of equality trumped states' rights; democratic majorities in individual states could not abridge the fundamental rights of people living within them. While Lincoln brought his country into war arguing for preservation of the Union, he understood from the beginning that the real issue was slavery and the threat it represented to the founding principle of equality.* This broader understanding of identity was the "new birth of freedom" that he referred to in the Gettysburg Address.[19]

The defeat of the South in the Civil War widened the sense of American peoplehood through the Thirteenth Amendment, which abolished slavery; the Fourteenth Amendment, which defined citizenship to include all people born or naturalized in the territory of the United States (the jus soli), and gave them an equal right to due process; and the Fifteenth Amendment, which prohibited denial of the right to vote based on race, color, or previous condition of servitude. Shamefully, the promise of these amendments would not be fulfilled until the civil rights era a hundred years later, and even today it is being threatened by measures seeking to restrict the franchise among minority voters. Yet the principle of a nonracially based national identity was clearly articulated, as well as the power of the federal government to enforce the underlying rights of Americans. It has become part of the way that most Americans think of themselves.

By the middle of the twentieth century, the de facto diver-

---

* As Lincoln said in his second inaugural address, "One-eighth of the whole population were colored slaves, not distributed generally over the Union, but localized in the Southern part of it. These slaves constituted a peculiar and powerful interest. All knew that this interest was, somehow, the cause of the war."

sity of the United States made it impossible to define American peoplehood in either religious or ethnic terms. Following the massive wave of immigration at the turn of the twentieth century, the percentage of foreign-born Americans had risen to about 15 percent of the whole population. Too many of them and their children fell outside traditional religious or ethnic categories for politicians to speak as they once did of the United States as a "Christian" or an "Anglo-Saxon" nation. Of John Jay's four characteristics of peoplehood—shared religion, shared ethnicity, shared language, and shared commitment to common principles of government—only the latter two, language and common devotion to democratic government, remained.* This represented the "creedal" understanding of American identity referred to by Senator Sasse.

This creedal understanding of American identity emerged as the result of a long struggle stretching over nearly two centuries and represented a decisive break with earlier versions of identity based on race, ethnicity, or religion. Americans can be proud of this very substantive identity; it is based on belief in the common political principles of constitutionalism, the rule of law, democratic accountability, and the principle that "all men are created equal" (now interpreted to include all women). These political ideas come directly out of the Enlightenment and are the only possible basis for unifying a modern liberal democracy that has become de facto multicultural.

The type of identity politics increasingly practiced on both the left and the right is deeply problematic because it returns to understandings of identity based on fixed characteristics such

---

* The English language remains an important integrative characteristic of American identity, which is why bi- and multilingual programs in public schools have been controversial.

as race, ethnicity, and religion, which had earlier been defeated at great cost.

On the left, proponents of narrow identity politics assert that the U.S. identity is its diversity, or that we are somehow united by our diversity. Others have argued that the United States is too diverse to have a national identity, and that we shouldn't worry about it one way or the other. In light of the populist understandings of identity that have lately arisen, it is understandable why people retreat to diversity as a virtue. To say that the United States is a diverse society is true. But diversity cannot be the basis for identity in and of itself; it is like saying that our identity is to have no identity; or rather, that we should get used to our having nothing in common and emphasize our narrow ethnic or racial identities instead.

On the right, some have retreated into earlier versions of identity based on race and religion. Former Republican vice-presidential candidate Sarah Palin once characterized "real Americans" as those residing in small towns and rural areas, something that deliberately excluded the diverse populations of U.S. cities. Donald Trump has taken this view to new heights, awakening an ugly form of populist nationalism that would reassert an ethnic or religious understanding of the country. As he said at one campaign rally in 2016, "The only important thing is the unification of the people" because "the other people don't mean anything."[20] This implies in practice that the "real people" expel or somehow forcibly exclude the "other people" from civic life—not a formula for national unity, but for civil war.

Many theorists of modern democracy have argued that passive acceptance of a democratic creed is not enough to make such a system work. Democracies require certain positive virtues on the part of citizens as well. Alexis de Tocqueville in particular warned of the temptation of people in democratic societies to turn inward and preoccupy themselves with their own welfare and that of their families exclusively. Successful democracy, according to him, requires citizens who are patriotic, informed, active, public-spirited, and willing to participate in political matters. In this age of polarization, one might add that they should be open-minded, tolerant of other viewpoints, and ready to compromise their own views for the sake of democratic consensus.

Samuel Huntington was one of the few contemporary political thinkers to make an argument that the success of the United States as a nation depended not just on a minimal creedal understanding of identity, but on certain cultural norms and virtues as well. In his final book, *Who Are We?*, he famously asked, "Would America be the America it is today if in the seventeenth and eighteenth centuries it had been settled not by British Protestants but by French, Spanish, or Portuguese Catholics? The answer is no. It would not be America; it would be Quebec, Mexico, or Brazil."[21] He talked about what he called Anglo-Protestant culture as a necessary component of American identity, a culture that was built around the Protestant work ethic.

Huntington was denounced as a racist and, more recently, as an academic precursor to Donald Trump.[22] A proper understanding of Huntington's argument, however, would exonerate him of charges of racism, even if one disagreed with his policy prescriptions on immigration.

Huntington was not making an argument for an Anglo-Protestant understanding of American identity if that meant that only Anglo-Saxon Protestants could qualify as Americans. Rather, he was saying that the Anglo-Protestant settlers to the United States brought with them a culture that was critical for the subsequent development of the country as a successful democracy. The culture is important, not the ethnic or religious identities of those who take part in it. His view is, in my opinion, undeniably true.

One of the elements of that culture that Huntington emphasized was the "Protestant" work ethic. Empirically, Americans do work much harder than many other peoples around the world—less hard than many Asians, but certainly harder than most Europeans.[23] The historical origins of this work ethic may indeed lie in the Puritanism of the country's early settlers, but who in the United States works hard these days? It is just as likely to be a Korean grocery-store owner or an Ethiopian cab-driver or a Mexican gardener as a person of Anglo-Protestant heritage living off dividends in his or her country club. While we can acknowledge the historical roots of this culture, we must also recognize that it has become detached from its particular ethno-religious origins to become the common property of all Americans.

Huntington was, in my view, wrong to fear that Mexican immigrants would not eventually adopt Anglo-Protestant values and habits. Empirically, this worry would seem to be overblown. He was more justified in his concern that contemporary understandings of multiculturalism and identity politics were putting up unnecessary barriers to assimilation, barriers that did not exist for earlier generations of immigrants.

The question is not whether Americans should go backward into an ethnic and religious understanding of identity. The contemporary fate of the United States—and that of any other culturally diverse democracy that wants to survive—is to be a creedal nation. But it also needs an understanding of positive virtues, not bound to particular groups, that are needed to make that democracy work. While it would be wrong today to link identity to race, ethnicity, or religion, it is correct to say that national identity in a well-functioning democracy requires something more than passive acceptance of a creed. It requires citizenship and the exercise of certain virtues. A creedal identity is a necessary but not a sufficient condition for success.

14

WHAT IS TO BE DONE?

We cannot get away from identity or identity politics. Identity is the "powerful moral idea that has come down to us," in Charles Taylor's phrase, and it has crossed borders and cultures since it builds on the universal human psychology of thymos. This moral idea tells us that we have authentic inner selves that are not being recognized and suggests that the whole of external society may be false and repressive. It focuses our natural demand for recognition of our dignity and gives us a language for expressing the resentments that arise when such recognition is not forthcoming.

That the demand for dignity should somehow disappear is neither possible nor desirable. It was the spark that ignited countless popular protests, from the French Revolution to that of the disrespected street vendor in Tunisia. These people wanted to be treated like adults, adults who were able to influence the governments that lorded over them. Liberal democracy is built around the rights given to individuals who are equal in their freedom, that is, who have an equal degree of choice and agency in determining their collective political lives.

But many people are not satisfied with simple equal recognition as generic human beings. The rights one enjoys as a citizen of a democracy are highly valued when one lives under a dictatorship, but come to be taken for granted over time once democracy has been established. Unlike their parents, young people growing up in Eastern Europe today have no personal experience of life under communism, and can take the liberties they enjoy for granted. This allows them to focus on other things: the hidden potentialities that are not being permitted to flourish and the way that they are being held back by the social norms and institutions around them.

Being a citizen of a liberal democracy does not mean, moreover, that people will actually be treated with equal respect either by their government or by other citizens. They are judged on the basis of their skin color, their gender, their national origin, their looks, their ethnicity, or their sexual orientation. Each person and each group experiences disrespect in different ways, and each seeks its own dignity. Identity politics thus engenders its own dynamic, by which societies divide themselves into smaller and smaller groups by virtue of their particular "lived experience" of victimization.

Confusion over identity arises as a condition of living in the modern world. Modernization means constant change and disruption, and the opening up of choices that did not exist before. It is mobile, fluid, and complex. This fluidity is by and large a good thing: over generations, millions of people have been fleeing villages and traditional societies that do not offer them choices, in favor of ones that do.

But the freedom and degree of choice that exist in a modern liberal society can also leave people unhappy and disconnected from their fellow human beings. They find themselves nostalgic for the community and structured life they think they have lost, or that their ancestors supposedly once possessed. The authentic identities they are seeking are ones that bind them to other people. They can be seduced by leaders who tell them that they have been betrayed and disrespected by the existing power structures, and that they are members of important communities whose greatness will again be recognized.

Many modern liberal democracies find themselves at the cusp of an important choice. They have had to accommodate rapid economic and social change and have become far more diverse as a result of globalization. This has created demands for recognition on the part of groups who were previously invisible to the mainstream society. But this has entailed a perceived lowering of the status of the groups they have displaced, leading to a politics of resentment and backlash. The retreat on both sides into ever narrower identities threatens the possibility of deliberation and collective action by the society as a whole. Down this road lies, ultimately, state breakdown and failure.

The nature of modern identity is to be changeable, however. While some individuals may persuade themselves that their identity is based on their biology and is outside their control, the condition of modernity is to have multiple identities, ones that are shaped by our social interactions on any number of levels. We have identities defined by our race, gender, workplace, education, affinities, and nation. For many teenagers, identity forms around the specific subgenre of music that they and their friends listen to.

But if the logic of identity politics is to divide societies into ever smaller, self-regarding groups, it is also possible to create identities that are broader and more integrative. One does not have to deny the potentialities and lived experiences of individuals to recognize that they can also share values and aspirations with much broader circles of citizens. *Erlebnis* can aggregate into *Erfahrung*; lived experience can become just plain experience. So while we will never get away from identity politics in the modern world, we can steer it back to broader forms of mutual respect for dignity that will make democracy more functional.

How do we translate these abstract ideas into concrete policies at the current moment? We can start by trying to counter the specific abuses that have driven assertions of identity, such as unwarranted police violence against minorities or sexual assault and sexual harrassment in workplaces, schools, and other institutions. No critique of identity politics should imply that these are not real and urgent problems that need concrete solutions.

Beyond that, there is a larger agenda of integrating smaller groups into larger wholes on which trust and citizenship can be based. We need to promote creedal national identities built around the foundational ideas of modern liberal democracy, and use public policies to deliberately assimilate newcomers to those identities. Liberal democracy has its own culture, which must be held in higher esteem than cultures rejecting democracy's values.

Over recent decades, the European left had come to support a form of multiculturalism that downplayed the importance of integrating immigrants into the national culture. Under the banner of antiracism it looked the other way from evidence that assimilation wasn't working. The new populist right, for its part, looks back nostalgically at a fading national culture that was based on ethnicity or religion, a culture that was largely free of immigrants or significant diversities.

In the United States, identity politics has fractured the left into a series of identity groups that are home to its most energetic political activists. It has in many respects lost touch with the one identity group that used to be its largest constituency, the white working class. This has spawned the rise of a populist right that feels its own identity to be under threat, abetted by a president whose personal vanity is tied to the degree of anger and polarization he can stoke.

The European agenda must start with redefinitions of national identity embodied in its citizenship laws. Ideally, the EU should create a single citizenship whose requirements would be based on adherence to basic liberal democratic principles, one that would supersede national citizenship laws. This has not been politically possible in the past, and it is much less thinkable now with the rise of populist parties across the Continent. It would help if the EU democratized itself by shifting powers from the Commission to the Parliament and tried to make up for lost time by investing in European identity through the creation of the appropriate symbols and narratives that would be inculcated through a common educational system. This too is likely to be beyond the capability of a union of twenty-eight members, each of which remains jealous of its national prerogatives and stands ready to veto such a program. Any action that takes place will therefore have to happen, for better or worse, on a member-state level.

Those laws of EU member states still based on jus sanguinis need to be changed to jus soli so as not to privilege one ethnic group over another. It is perfectly legitimate to impose stringent requirements for the naturalization of new citizens, something the United States has done for many years. In the United

States, in addition to proving continuous residency in the country for five years, new citizens are expected to be able to read, write, and speak basic English, to have an understanding of U.S. history and government, to be of good moral character (i.e., no criminal record), and to demonstrate an attachment to the principles and ideals of the U.S. Constitution. The latter is undertaken by swearing the naturalization oath of allegiance to the United States of America:

> I hereby declare, on oath, that I absolutely and entirely renounce and abjure all allegiance and fidelity to any foreign prince, potentate, state, or sovereignty, of whom or which I have heretofore been a subject or citizen; that I will support and defend the Constitution and laws of the United States of America against all enemies, foreign and domestic; that I will bear true faith and allegiance to the same; that I will bear arms on behalf of the United States when required by the law; that I will perform noncombatant service in the Armed Forces of the United States when required by the law; that I will perform work of national importance under civilian direction when required by the law; and that I take this obligation freely, without any mental reservation or purpose of evasion; so help me God.[1]

Dual citizenship has become increasingly widespread today as migration levels have increased. For many people who travel or have family in different countries, having multiple passports is a great convenience. But if one takes national identity seriously, it is a rather questionable practice. Different nations have different identities and different interests that can engender potentially conflicting allegiances. The most obvious problem involves military service: if the two countries of which one is a citizen go to war with each other, one's loyalties are automatically in question. This may seem a moot issue with the reduced likelihood of war in most of the world, but we unfortunately cannot assume that military conflict will not occur in the future. Even short of such contingencies, dual citizenship raises serious political problems. In Germany's 2017 election, for example, Turkey's authoritarian president, Recep Tayyip Erdoğan, encouraged German citizens of Turkish origin to vote for politicians who would favor Turkish interests, rather than voting for those they thought were best for Germany. Those who were citizens of both countries might have a harder time deciding how to vote than those who had forsworn loyalty to Turkey.[2]

In addition to changing the formal requirements for citizenship, European countries need to shift their popular understandings of national identity away from those based on ethnicity. In the early 2000s, a German academic of Syrian origin named Bassam Tibi proposed *Leitkultur*, "leading culture," as the basis for German national identity.[3] *Leitkultur* was defined in liberal Enlightenment terms as belief in equality and democratic values. Yet his proposal was attacked from the left for suggesting that those values were superior to other cultural values; in doing so the left gave unwitting comfort not just to Islamists, but also to the right that still believed in ethnic identity. Germany needs something precisely like *Leitkultur*, a normative change that would permit a Turk to speak of him- or herself as German. This is beginning to happen, but slowly.[4]

Down the road, something like a pan-European identity may someday emerge. Perhaps this needs to happen outside the cumbersome and bureaucratic decision-making structures that constitute the contemporary EU. Europeans have created a remarkable civilization of which they should be proud, one that can encompass people from other cultures even as it remains aware of the distinctiveness of its own.

Compared to Europe, the United States has been far more welcoming of immigrants because it developed a creedal identity early on, based on its long history of immigration. Compared to Europeans, Americans have been proud of their naturalized citizens and typically make a great deal out of the naturalization ceremony, with color guards and hopeful speeches by local politicians. As the political scientist Seymour Martin Lipset used to point out, in the United States one can be accused of being "un-American" in a way that one could not be said to be "un-Danish" or "un-Japanese." Americanism constituted a set of beliefs and a way of life, not an ethnicity; one can deviate from the former but not the latter.

The creedal national identity that emerged in the wake of the American Civil War today needs to be strongly reemphasized and defended from attacks by both the left and the right. On the right, plenty of new white nationalist voices would like to drag the country backward to an identity once again based on race, ethnicity, or religion. It is urgent that these views be firmly rejected as un-American, much as Ben Sasse sought to do.

On the left, identity politics has sought to undermine the legitimacy of the American national story by emphasizing victimization, insinuating in some cases that racism, gender discrimination, and other forms of systematic exclusion are somehow intrinsic to the country's DNA. All these things have been and continue to be features of American society, and they need to be confronted in the present. But a progressive narrative can also be told about the overcoming of barriers and the ever-broadening circles of people whose dignity the country has recognized, based on its founding principles. This narrative was part of the "new birth of freedom" envisioned by Abraham Lincoln, and one that Americans celebrate on the holiday he created, Thanksgiving.

While the United States has benefited from diversity, it cannot build its national identity around diversity as such. Identity has to be related to substantive ideas such as constitutionalism, rule of law, and human equality. Americans respect these ideas; the country is justified in excluding from citizenship those who reject them.

Once a country has defined a proper creedal identity that is open to the de facto diversity of modern societies, the nature of controversies over immigration will inevitably have to change. In both Europe and the United States, that debate is currently polarized between a right that seeks to cut off immigration altogether and would like to send current immigrants back to their countries of origin and a left that asserts a virtually unlimited obligation on the part of liberal democracies to accept migrants. The real focus should instead be on strategies for better assimilating immigrants to a country's creedal identity. Well-assimilated immigrants bring a healthy diversity to any society, and the benefits of immigration can be fully realized. Poorly assimilated immigrants are a drag on the state and in some cases constitute dangerous security threats.

Europeans pay lip service to the need for better assimilation, but fail to follow through with an effective set of policies. The reform agenda here is highly varied since individual European countries approach the problem very differently. Many countries have in place policies that actively impede integration, such as the Dutch system of pillarization. Britain and a number of other European countries provide public funding for Muslim schools, just as they support Christian and Jewish schools. To some extent this simply reflects the geographical concentration of immigrant communities, and was done in the name of equal treatment. If assimilation is the goal, however, this whole structure should be replaced by a system of common schools teaching a standardized curriculum. As in the Netherlands, it is a reach to think that this would be politically feasible, yet that is the kind of approach that would be needed were countries to take integration seriously.[5]

In France, the problem is somewhat different. The French concept of republican citizenship, like its American counterpart, is creedal, built around the ideals of liberty, equality, and fraternity coming out of the French Revolution. The 1905 law on *laïcité* formally separates church and state and makes impossible the kinds of publicly funded religious schools operating in Britain or the Netherlands.[6] The French problem is threefold. First, whatever French law says, a lot of discrimination in French society remains, which holds back opportunities from immigrants. Second, the French economy has been underperforming for years, leading to overall unemployment rates that are twice those of neighboring Germany. For France's immigrant youth, the numbers are reaching 35 percent, compared to 25 for French youth as a whole. One important thing that France needs to do to integrate immigrants is to get them jobs and increase their hope for a better future, for instance by liberalizing the labor market, as Emmanuel Macron has sought to do. Finally, the very idea of French national identity and French culture has been under attack as Islamophobic; assimilation itself is not politically acceptable to many on the left. Defense of republican ideals of universal citizenship should not be left to parties like the National Front.

In the United States, an assimilation agenda begins with public education. The teaching of basic civics has been in long-term decline in the United States, not just for immigrants but for native-born Americans, and this needs to be reversed. Like Europe, the United States too has policies that impede assimilation, such as the thirteen or so different languages taught in the New York City public school system. Bi- and multilingual programs have been marketed as ways of speeding the acquisition of the English language by nonnative speakers. But it has developed a constituency of its own, with the educational bureaucracy defending its prerogatives regardless of actual outcomes for English acquisition.[7]

Assimilation of immigrants may require even more active measures. In recent decades, courts in the United States and other developed democracies have gradually eroded the distinction between citizen and noncitizen.[8] Noncitizens rightfully enjoy many legal rights, including rights to due process, speech, association, free exercise of religion, and a range of state services such as education. Noncitizens also share duties with citizens: they are expected to obey the law and must pay taxes, though only citizens are liable for jury duty in the United States. The distinction between noncitizens who are documented and those who are not is sharper, since the latter are liable to deportation, but even the undocumented possess due process rights. The only major right that is conveyed solely by citizenship is the right to vote; in addition, citizens can enter and exit the country freely and can expect support from their government when traveling abroad.

Small as they are, it is important to hold on to these distinctions. Basic human rights are universal, but full enjoyment of rights actively enforced by state power is a reward for membership in a national community and acceptance of that community's rules. The right to vote is particularly important, since it gives individuals a share of state power. As a human being, I may have an abstract right to citizenship and political representation, but as an American citizen I would not expect to be able to vote in Italy or in Ghana, even if I lived in one of those countries.

Contemporary liberal democracies do not demand a lot in return for state protection of their citizens' rights, and in particular the right to vote. The sense of national community might be strengthened by a universal requirement for national service. Such a mandate would underline the fact that citizenship requires commitment and sacrifice to maintain. One could do it by serving either in the military or in a civilian capacity. This requirement is actually articulated in the American naturalization oath, which enjoins willingness to bear arms on behalf of the country, or to work in a civilian service as required by law. If such service was correctly structured, it would force young people to work together with others from very different social classes, regions, races, and ethnicities, just as military service does today. And like all forms of shared sacrifice, it would be a powerful way of integrating newcomers into the national culture. National service would be a contemporary form of classical republicanism, a form of democracy that encouraged virtue and public-spiritedness rather than simply leaving citizens alone to pursue their private lives.

A policy focus on assimilation also means that levels of immigration and rates of change become important, for both Europe and the United States. Assimilation into a dominant culture becomes much harder as the numbers of immigrants rise relative to the native population. As immigrant communities reach a certain scale, they tend to become self-sufficient and no longer need connections to the groups outside themselves. They can overwhelm public services and strain the capacity of schools and other public institutions to care for them. While immigrants will likely have a positive net effect on public finance in the long run, this will happen only if they get jobs and become taxpaying citizens or legal resident aliens. Large numbers of newcomers can also weaken support for generous welfare benefits on the part of native-born citizens, a factor in both the European and the American immigration debates.

Liberal democracies benefit greatly from immigration, both economically and culturally. But they also unquestionably have the right to control their own borders. A democratic political system is based on a contract between government and citizen in which both have obligations. Such a contract makes no sense without delimitation of citizenship and exercise of the franchise. All people have a basic human right to citizenship, something that, according to the Universal Declaration of Human Rights, cannot be arbitrarily taken away from them. But that does not mean they have the right to citizenship in any particular country. International law does not, moreover, challenge the right of states to control their borders, or to set criteria for citizenship.[9] What refugees are owed is sympathy, compassion, and support. Like all moral obligations, however, these obligations need to be tempered by practical considerations of scarce resources, competing priorities, and the political sustainability of a program of support.

For Europe, this implies that the EU as a whole needs to be able to control its external borders better than it does, which in practice means giving countries such as Italy and Greece both material help and stronger authority to regulate the flow of migrants into Europe. The organization charged with doing this, Frontex, is understaffed, underfunded, and lacks strong political support from the very member states most concerned with keeping migrants out. The Schengen system of free internal movement will not be politically sustainable unless the problem of Europe's outer borders is somehow solved.

The situation in the United States is somewhat different. The country has been very inconsistent in the enforcement of its immigration laws over the years. This enforcement is not impossible, but is a matter of political will. While levels of deportations began rising under the Obama administration, the often arbitrary nature of these actions does not make for a sustainable long-term policy. Enforcement does not require a border wall; a huge proportion of undocumented aliens have entered the country legally but have remained on expired visas. Rather, the rules could be better enforced through a system of employer sanctions, which requires a national identification system that will tell employers who is legitimately in the country. This has not happened because too many employers benefit from the cheap labor that immigrants provide and do not want to act as enforcement agents. It has also not come about because of a uniquely American opposition to a national ID system, based on a suspicion of government shared by left and right alike.

As a result, the United States now hosts a population of some 11–12 million undocumented aliens. The vast majority of these people have been in the country for years and are doing useful work, raising families, and otherwise behaving as law-abiding citizens. The idea that they are all criminals because they violated U.S. law to enter the country is ridiculous, though some within this population are criminals, just as within the native-born population. It is also ridiculous to think that the United States could ever force all these people to leave the country and return to their countries of origin. A project on that scale would be worthy of Stalin's Soviet Union or Nazi Germany.

So the possibility of a basic bargain on immigration reform has existed for some time. In a trade, the government would undertake serious enforcement measures to control its borders, in return for an agreement to give undocumented aliens without criminal records a path toward citizenship.[10] This bargain might actually receive majority support among the American public, but hard-core immigration opponents are dead set against any form of "amnesty," and pro-immigrant groups are opposed to stricter enforcement of existing rules. The polarization and dysfunction of the American political system has made this bargain unachievable for many years. I have elsewhere labeled instances of this sort American vetocracy, by which minority views can easily block majority consensus.[11]

If the United States is serious about assimilating immigrants, then it needs to reform its immigration system along the lines just outlined. Acquiring U.S. citizenship and swearing the naturalization oath are critical and poignant markers of assimilation. Some object that giving undocumented aliens a path to citizenship rewards them for breaking U.S. law and allows them to jump the queue ahead of legal aliens seeking naturalization. A public service requirement might help ease such concerns. The country is creating an unnecessary obstacle to assimilation under the fantasy that the millions of undocumented aliens living peacefully and productively in the country will ultimately be deported back to their countries of origin. Meanwhile, America's inability to enforce existing laws ensures that this problem will persist.

Public policies that focus on the successful assimilation of foreigners might help take the wind out of the sails of the current populist upsurge both in Europe and in the United States. The new groups vociferously opposing immigration are actually coalitions of people with different concerns. A hard-core group are driven by racism and bigotry; little can be done to change their minds. They should not be catered to, but simply opposed on moral grounds. But others are concerned whether newcomers will ultimately assimilate. They worry less about there being immigration than about numbers, speed of change, and the carrying capacity of existing institutions to accommodate these changes. A policy focus on assimilation might ease their concerns and peel them away from the simple bigots. Whether or not this happens, a policy focusing on assimilation would be good for national cohesion.

Policies related to immigrants, refugees, and citizenship are at the heart of current identity debates, but the issue is much broader than that. Identity politics is rooted in a world in which the poor and marginalized are invisible to their peers, as Adam Smith remarked. Resentment over lost status starts with real economic distress, and one way of muting the resentment is to mitigate concerns over jobs, incomes, and security.

Particularly in the United States, much of the left stopped thinking several decades ago about ambitious social policies that might help remedy the underlying conditions of the poor. It was easier to talk about respect and dignity than to come up with potentially costly plans that would concretely reduce inequality. A major exception was President Obama, whose Affordable Care Act was a milestone in U.S. social policy. The ACA's opponents tried to frame it as an identity issue, suggesting sotto voce that the policy was designed by a black president to help his black constituents. But it was in fact a national policy designed to help less well-off Americans, regardless of their race or identity. Many of the law's beneficiaries include rural whites in the South who have nonetheless been persuaded to vote for Republican politicians vowing to repeal the ACA.

Identity politics has made the crafting of such ambitious policies more difficult. For much of the twentieth century, politics in liberal democracies revolved around broad economic policy issues. The progressive left wanted to protect ordinary people from the vagaries of the market, and to use the power of the state to more fairly distribute resources. The right for its part wanted to protect the free enterprise system and the ability of everyone to participate in market exchange. Communist, socialist, social democratic, liberal, and conservative parties all arrayed themselves on a spectrum from left to right that could be measured by the desired degree of state intervention, and commitment alternatively to equality or to individual freedom. There were important identity groups as well, including parties whose agendas were nationalist, religious, or regional in scope. But the stability of democratic politics in the period from the end of World War II up to the present revolved around dominant center-left and center-right parties that largely agreed on the legitimacy of a democratic welfare state.

This consensus now represents an old establishment that is being hotly contested by new parties firmly rooted in identity issues. This constitutes a big challenge for the future of democratic politics. While fights over economic policy produced sharp polarization early in the twentieth century, democracies found that opposing economic visions could often split the difference and compromise. Identity issues, by contrast, are harder to reconcile: either you recognize me or you don't. Resentment over lost dignity or invisibility often has economic roots, but fights over identity often distract us from focusing on policies that could concretely remedy those issues. In countries such as the United States, South Africa, or India, with racial, ethnic, and religious stratifications, it has been harder to create broad working-class coalitions to fight for redistribution because the higher-status identity groups did not want to make common cause with those below them, and vice versa.

The rise of the politics of identity has been facilitated by technological change. When the internet first became a platform for mass communication in the 1990s, many observers (myself included) believed that it would be an important force for promoting democratic values. Information is a form of power, and if the internet increased everyone's access to information, it should also have distributed power more broadly. Moreover, the rise of social media in particular seemed likely to be a useful mobilization tool, allowing like-minded groups to coalesce around issues of common concern. The peer-to-peer nature of the internet would eliminate the tyranny of hierarchical gatekeepers of all sorts, who curated the nature of information to which people had access.

And so it was: any number of antiauthoritarian uprisings, from the Rose and Orange Revolutions in Georgia and Ukraine to the failed Green Revolution in Iran to the Tunisian revolt and the Tahrir Square uprising in Egypt, were powered by social media and the internet. Government operations were much harder to keep secret once ordinary people had technological means of publicizing abuses; Black Lives Matter would likely not have taken off in the absence of ubiquitous cell phones and video recordings.

But over time, authoritarian governments such as that of China figured out how to control use of the internet for their own populations and to make it politically harmless, while Russia learned how to turn social media into a weapon that would weaken its democratic rivals.[12] But even absent these external players, social media has succeeded in accelerating the fragmentation of liberal societies by playing into the hands of identity groups. It connected like-minded people with one another, freed from the tyranny of geography. It permitted them to communicate, and to wall themselves off from people and views that they didn't like, in "filter bubbles." In most face-to-face communities, the number of people believing a given outlandish conspiracy theory would be very limited; online, one could discover thousands of fellow believers. By undermining traditional media's editors, fact-checkers, and professional codes, it facilitated the circulation of bad information and deliberate efforts to smear and undermine political opponents. And its anonymity removed existing restraints on civility. Not only did it support society's willingness to see itself in identity terms; it promoted new identities through online communities, as countless subreddits have done.

Fears about the future are often best expressed through fiction, particularly science fiction that tries to imagine future worlds based on new kinds of technology. In the first half of the twentieth century, many of those forward-looking fears centered around big, centralized, bureaucratic tyrannies that snuffed out individuality and privacy. George Orwell's *1984* foresaw Big Brother controlling individuals through the telescreen, while Aldous Huxley's *Brave New World* saw the state using biotechnology to stratify and control society. But the nature of imagined dystopias began to change in the later decades of the century, when environmental collapse and out-of-control viruses took center stage.

However, one particular strand spoke to the anxieties raised by identity politics. Cyberpunk authors such as Bruce Sterling, William Gibson, and Neal Stephenson saw a future dominated not by centralized dictatorships, but by uncontrolled social fragmentation that was facilitated by a new emerging technology called the internet. Stephenson's 1992 novel *Snow Crash* posited a ubiquitous virtual "metaverse" in which individuals could adopt avatars, interact, and change their identities at will. The United States had broken down into "burbclaves," suburban subdivisions catering to narrow identities such as New

South Africa for the racists with their Confederate flags, or Mr. Lee's Greater Hong Kong for Chinese immigrants. Passports and visas were required to travel from one neighborhood to the other. The CIA was privatized, and the USS *Enterprise* had become a floating home for refugees. The authority of the federal government shrank to encompass only the land on which federal buildings were located.[13]

Our present world is simultaneously moving toward the opposing dystopias of hypercentralization and endless fragmentation. China, for instance, is building a massive dictatorship in which the government collects data on the daily transactions of every one of its citizens and uses big-data techniques and a social credit system to control its population. On the other hand, different parts of the world are seeing the breakdown of centralized institutions, the emergence of failed states, polarization, and a growing lack of consensus over common ends. Social media and the internet have facilitated the emergence of self-contained communities, walled off not by physical barriers but by belief in shared identity.

The nice thing about dystopian fiction is that it almost never comes true. That we can imagine how current trends will play themselves out in an ever more exaggerated fashion serves as a useful warning: *1984* became a potent symbol of a totalitarian future we wanted to avoid and helped inoculate us from it. We can imagine better places to be in, which take account of our societies' increasing diversity, yet present a vision for how that diversity will still serve common ends and support rather than undermine liberal democracy.

Identity is the theme that underlies many political phenomena today, from new populist nationalist movements, to Islamist fighters, to the controversies taking place on university campuses. We will not escape from thinking about ourselves and our society in identity terms. But we need to remember that the identities dwelling deep inside us are neither fixed nor necessarily given to us by our accidents of birth. Identity can be used to divide, but it can and has also been used to integrate. That in the end will be the remedy for the populist politics of the present.

NOTES

Preface

1. Francis Fukuyama, "The Populist Surge," *The American Interest* 13 (4) (2018): 16–18.
2. Larry Diamond, "Facing Up to the Democratic Recession," *Journal of Democracy* 26 (1) (2015): 141–55.
3. Francis Fukuyama, "The End of History?," *National Interest* 16 (Summer 1989): 3–18; *The End of History and the Last Man* (New York: Free Press, 1992).
4. I am interpreting Hegel through the lens of Alexandre Kojève, who saw the evolving European Economic Community as the embodiment of the end of history.
5. Francis Fukuyama, *The Origins of Political Order: From Prehuman Times to the French Revolution* (New York: Farrar, Straus and Giroux, 2011); *Political Order and Political Decay: From the Industrial Revolution to the Globalization of Democracy* (New York: Farrar, Straus and Giroux, 2014).
6. I am grateful to those people who actually took the time to read my book. See in particular Paul Sagar, "The Last Hollow Laugh," *Aeon*, March 21, 2017, https://aeon.co/essays/was-francis-fukuyama-the-first -man-to-see-trump-coming.
7. Seymour Martin Lipset Lecture; see Francis Fukuyama, "Identity, Immigration, and Liberal Democracy," *Journal of Democracy* 17 (2) (2006):

5–20; Latsis lecture "European Identity Challenges," given at the University of Geneva in November 2011, see "The Challenges for European Identity," *Global*, January 11, 2012, http://www.theglobaljournal.net /group/francis-fukuyama/article/469/.

1. The Politics of Dignity

1. Samuel P. Huntington, *The Third Wave: Democratization in the Late Twentieth Century* (Oklahoma City: University of Oklahoma Press, 1991).
2. Steven Radelet, *The Great Surge: The Ascent of the Developing World* (New York: Simon and Schuster, 2015), 4.
3. For a comprehensive account of the growth of global inequality, see Branko Milanovic, *Global Inequality: A New Approach for the Age of Globalization* (Cambridge, MA: Belknap Press, 2016).
4. Diamond, "Facing Up to the Democratic Recession," 141–55.
5. Ali Alichi, Kory Kantenga, and Juan Solé, "Income Polarization in the United States," IMF Working Paper WP/16/121 (Washington, DC, 2017); Thomas Piketty and Emmanuel Saez, "Income Inequality in the United States, 1913–1998," *Quarterly Journal of Economics* 118 (1) (2003): 1–39.
6. Viktor Orbán, "Will Europe Belong to Europeans?," speech given in Baile Tusnad, Romania, July 22, 2017, *Visegrád Post*, July 24, 2017, https:// visegradpost.com/en/2017/07/24/full-speech-of-v-orban-will-europe -belong-to-europeans/.
7. Rukmini Callimachi, "Terrorist Groups Vow Bloodshed over Jerusalem. ISIS? Less So," *New York Times*, December 8, 2017.
8. Orbán, "Will Europe Belong?"
9. James D. Fearon, "What Is Identity (As We Now Use the Word)?," unpublished paper, November 3, 1999, http://fearonresearch.stanford .edu/53-2.

2. The Third Part of the Soul

1. Daniel Kahneman, *Thinking, Fast and Slow* (New York: Farrar, Straus and Giroux, 2013).
2. *The Republic of Plato*, trans., with notes and an interpretive essay, by Allan Bloom (New York: Basic Books, 1968), variorum sec. 439b–c.
3. Ibid., 439e–440a.
4. Ibid., 440a–b.

5. Ibid., 440e–441a.
6. For an account of how isothymia plays out in practice, see Robert W. Fuller, *Somebodies and Nobodies: Overcoming the Abuse of Rank* (Gabriola Island, British Columbia: New Society Publishers, 2003).
7. Robert H. Frank, *Choosing the Right Pond: Human Behavior and the Quest for Status* (Oxford: Oxford University Press, 1985), 7.

3. Inside and Outside

1. G. R. Elton, *Reformation Europe, 1517–1559* (New York: Harper Torchbooks, 1963), 2.
2. Martin Luther, *Christian Liberty*, ed. Harold J. Grimm (Philadelphia: Fortress Press, 1957), 7–8.
3. Charles Taylor, *Sources of the Self: The Making of the Modern Identity* (Cambridge, MA: Harvard University Press, 1989), 18.
4. Elton, *Reformation Europe*, 196.
5. See Taylor's *Sources of the Self* and *Multiculturalism: Examining the Politics of Recognition* (Princeton, NJ: Princeton University Press, 1994).
6. See Arthur M. Melzer, *The Natural Goodness of Man: On the System of Rousseau's Thought* (Chicago: University of Chicago Press, 1990).
7. Jean-Jacques Rousseau, *Oeuvres complètes de Jean-Jacques Rousseau*, vol. 3 (Paris: Éditions de la Pléiade, 1966), 165–66. Author's translation.
8. Ibid., 165.
9. Jean-Jacques Rousseau, *Les rêveries du promeneur solitaire* (Paris: Éditions Garnier Frères, 1960), 17. Author's translation.
10. Charles Taylor, *The Ethics of Authenticity* (Cambridge, MA: Harvard University Press, 1992), 26.
11. Rousseau's belief that sex was natural but not the family does not seem to be true of behaviorally modern human beings. It is true, however, of modern chimpanzees and may well have been true of the presumed chimplike progenitor of modern humans.
12. For a more detailed treatment of this topic, see Fukuyama, *Origins of Political Order*, 26–38.
13. Frank, *Choosing the Right Pond*, 21–25.

4. From Dignity to Democracy

1. Alexandre Kojève, *Introduction à la lecture de Hegel* (Paris: Éditions Gallimard, 1947).

6. Expressive Individualism

1. Rex Glensy, "The Right to Dignity," *Columbia Human Rights Law Review* 43 (65) (2011): 65–142.
2. Samuel Moyn, "The Secret History of Constitutional Dignity," *Yale Human Rights and Development Journal* 17 (2) (2014): 39–73. The term *dignity* has entered into arguments over abortion, since the Catholic Church has maintained that human dignity begins at conception and constitutes an inviolable moral status.
3. Glensy ("Right to Dignity," 77) notes that the word *dignity* appears in Federalist No. 1 (by Hamilton), but only in conjunction with the status of high officials.
4. Taylor, *Ethics of Authenticity*, 29.
5. David F. Strauss, *The Life of Jesus, Critically Examined* (London: Chapman Brothers, 1846).
6. Planned Parenthood of Southeastern Pennsylvania v. Casey, 505 U.S. 833.

7. Nationalism and Religion

1. Johann Gottfried von Herder, *Reflections on the Philosophy of the History of Mankind* (Chicago: University of Chicago Press, 1968).
2. Ibid., 31.
3. Herder was no particular fan of the absolute monarchies of his day and did not believe they were more conducive to human happiness than the stateless societies of North America or Africa. See Johann Gottfried von Herder, *J. G. Herder on Social and Political Culture* (Cambridge: Cambridge University Press, 1969), 318–19.
4. Ernest Gellner, *Nations and Nationalism* (Ithaca, NY: Cornell University Press, 1983), 33, 35.
5. Fritz Stern, *The Politics of Cultural Despair: A Study in the Rise of German Ideology* (Berkeley: University of California Press, 1974), 19–20.
6. Ibid., 35–94 passim.
7. Olivier Roy, "France's Oedipal Islamist Complex," *Foreign Policy*, January 7, 2016; Olivier Roy, "Who Are the New Jihadis?," *Guardian*, April 13, 2017.
8. Richard Barrett, *Foreign Fighters in Syria* (New York: Soufan Group, 2014).
9. See Omer Taspinar, "ISIS Recruitment and the Frustrated Achiever," *Huffington Post*, March 25, 2015.
10. Gilles Kepel, *Terror in France: The Rise of Jihad in the West* (Princeton, NJ: Princeton University Press, 2017); Robert F. Worth, "The Professor

and the Jihadi," *New York Times*, April 5, 2017; Robert Zaretsky, "Radicalized Islam, or Islamicized Radicalism?," *Chronicle of Higher Education* 62 (37) (2016).

8. The Wrong Address

1. Sheri Berman, "The Lost Left," *Journal of Democracy* 27 (4) (2016): 69–76. See also "Rose Thou Art Sick," *Economist*, April 2, 2016.
2. Thomas Piketty, *Capital in the Twenty-First Century* (Cambridge, MA: Belknap Press, 2014), 20–25, 170–87.
3. The number of bi-billionaires, that is, individuals with wealth of $2 billion in 2013 dollars, increased fivefold from 1987 to 2013; their combined wealth is more than all of Africa's. Milanovic, *Global Inequality*, 41–45.
4. Ibid., 11.
5. Alichi, Kantenga, and Solé, "Income Polarization," 5.
6. Gellner, *Nations and Nationalism*, 124.

9. Invisible Man

1. Adam Smith, *The Theory of Moral Sentiments* (Indianapolis: Liberty Classics, 1982), 50–51.
2. Frank, *Choosing the Right Pond*, 26–30.
3. Ibid., 21–26. See also Francis Fukuyama, *Our Posthuman Future: Consequences of the Biotechnology Revolution* (New York: Farrar, Straus and Giroux, 2001), 41–56.
4. Kahneman, *Thinking, Fast and Slow*, 283–85.
5. Federico Ferrara, "The Psychology of Thailand's Domestic Political Conflict: Democracy, Social Identity, and the 'Struggle for Recognition'" (manuscript presented at the international workshop "Coup, King, Crisis: Thailand's Political Troubles and the Royal Succession," Shorenstein Asia-Pacific Research Center, Stanford University, January 24–25, 2017).
6. See inter alia William Julius Wilson, *The Truly Disadvantaged: The Inner City, the Underclass, and Public Policy* (Chicago: University of Chicago Press, 1988).
7. Charles Murray, *Coming Apart: The State of White America, 1960–2010* (New York: Crown Forum, 2010); Robert D. Putnam, *Our Kids: The American Dream in Crisis* (New York: Simon and Schuster, 2015).
8. Anne Case and Angus Deaton, "Rising Morbidity and Mortality in Midlife Among White Non-Hispanics in the Twenty-First Century,"

Proceedings of the National Academy of Sciences 112 (49) (December 8, 2015); "Mortality and Morbidity in the Twenty-First Century," *Brookings Papers on Economic Activity*, March 23–24, 2017.

9. U.S. Census Bureau, *Current Population Survey* online data tool.

10. Katherine J. Cramer, *The Politics of Resentment: Rural Consciousness and the Rise of Scott Walker* (Chicago: University of Chicago Press, 2016), 61.

11. Arlie Russell Hochschild, *Strangers in Their Own Land: Anger and Mourning on the American Right* (New York: New Press, 2016), 127.

12. Cramer, *Politics of Resentment*, 9.

13. Hochschild, *Strangers in Their Own Land*, 143.

10. The Democratization of Dignity

1. The human potential movement was promoted by the Esalen Institute, one of whose early directors was Virginia Satir, to whose memory the California task force's report is dedicated.

2. Abraham Maslow, *A Theory of Human Motivation* (New York: Start Publishing, 2012).

3. *Toward a State of Self-Esteem: The Final Report of the California Task Force to Promote Self-Esteem and Personal Social Responsibility* (Sacramento: California State Department of Education, January 1990), 18–19.

4. Ibid., 19, 24. The universal need for self-esteem is also asserted in Robert W. Fuller, *Dignity for All: How to Create a World Without Rankism* (Oakland, CA: Berrett-Koehler Publishers, 2008).

5. Philip Rieff, *The Triumph of the Therapeutic: Uses of Faith After Freud* (Chicago: University of Chicago Press, 1966), 4, 13.

6. For an overview see Katie Wright, *The Rise of the Therapeutic Society: Psychological Knowledge and the Contradictions of Cultural Change* (Washington, DC: New Academia Publishing, 2010), 13–28.

7. Lionel Trilling, *Sincerity and Authenticity* (Cambridge, MA: Harvard University Press, 1972), 142.

8. Christopher Lasch, *The Culture of Narcissism: American Life in an Age of Diminishing Expectations* (New York: Norton, 1978), 10, 13.

9. Frank Furedi, *Therapy Culture: Cultivating Vulnerability in an Uncertain Age* (London: Routledge, 2004), 4–5, 10.

10. Robert H. Schuller, *Self-Esteem: The New Reformation* (Waco, TX: Waco Books, 1982). Schuller's books fall in a longer American tradition of self-help literature by authors such as Norman Vincent Peale. See for example Schuller's *Success Is Never Ending, Failure Is Never Final: How to*

Achieve Lasting Success Even in the Most Difficult Times (New York: Bantam Books, 1990).

11. Bob DeWaay, *Redefining Christianity: Understanding the Purpose Driven Movement* (Springfield, MO: 21st Century Press, 2006).

12. Andrew J. Polsky, *The Rise of the Therapeutic State* (Princeton, NJ: Princeton University Press, 1991), 158–64.

13. Ibid., 199–200.

14. Quoted in Herbert Lindenberger, "On the Sacrality of Reading Lists: The Western Culture Debate at Stanford University," in *The History in Literature: On Value, Genre, Institutions* (New York: Columbia University Press, 1990), 151.

15. The overall trend of universities undertaking a therapeutic mission is described in Frank Furedi, "The Therapeutic University," *American Interest* 13 (1) (2017): 55–62.

11. From Identity to Identities

1. Donald Horowitz, *Ethnic Groups in Conflict* (Berkeley: University of California Press, 1985), 141–43.

2. Ta-Nehisi Coates, *Between the World and Me* (New York: Spiegel and Grau, 2015), 7–10.

3. Simone de Beauvoir, *The Second Sex* (New York: Alfred A. Knopf, 1953).

4. Stuart Jeffries, "Are Women Human?" (interview with Catharine MacKinnon), *Guardian*, April 12, 2006.

5. See Jacob Hoerger, "Lived Experience vs. Experience," *Medium*, October 24, 2016, https://medium.com/@jacobhoerger/lived-experience-vs -experience-2e467b6c2229.

6. These points are all made in Hoerger, ibid.

7. Kimberlé Williams Crenshaw, "Mapping the Margins: Intersectionality, Identity Politics, and Violence Against Women of Color," *Stanford Law Review* 43:1241–99, July 1991.

8. Mathieu Bock-Côté, *Le multiculturalisme comme religion politique* (Paris: Les Éditions du Cerf, 2016), 16–19.

9. Sasha Polakow-Suransky, *Go Back to Where You Came From: The Backlash Against Immigration and the Fate of Western Democracy* (New York: Nation Books, 2017), 23–24.

10. Theo Lochocki, "Germany's Left Is Committing Suicide by Identity Politics," *Foreign Policy*, January 23, 2018.

11. Maximillian Alvarez, "Cogito Zero Sum," *Baffler*, August 2, 2017, https:// thebaffler.com/the-poverty-of-theory/cogito-zero-sum-alvarez.

12. An example of this is the treatment of Rebecca Tuvel for her article "In Defense of Transracialism," published in *Hypatia: A Journal of Feminist Philosophy*, as described by Kelly Oliver in "If This is Feminism . . . ," *Philosophical Salon*, May 8, 2017, http://thephilosophicalsalon.com/if-this-is-feminism-its-been-hijacked-by-the-thought-police/. See also Kelly Oliver, "Education in an Age of Outrage," *New York Times*, October 16, 2017.

13. Mark Lilla, *The Once and Future Liberal: After Identity Politics* (New York: HarperCollins, 2017).

14. Thomas E. Mann and Norman J. Ornstein, *It's Even Worse Than It Looks: How the American Constitutional System Collided with the New Politics of Extremism* (New York: Basic Books, 2012).

15. Cultural appropriation refers to the efforts of someone of one race, ethnicity, or gender to make use of or profit from the culture of another group. In one notable case, a painting by artist Dana Schutz of Emmett Till's mutilated corpse led to demands that the painting be destroyed on the grounds that she was a white painter depicting a moment traumatic for black people. In another case an editor was forced to step down from his position at the Canadian Writers Union for a piece defending the right of white authors to create characters from minority or indigenous backgrounds. In both cases the individuals being criticized were themselves liberals trying their best to sympathetically understand the experiences and sufferings of people from minority backgrounds.

The text of Hannah Black's letter criticizing Dana Schutz is given at https://i-d.vice.com/en_uk/article/d3p84a/black-artists-urge-the-whitney-biennial-to-remove-painting-of-murdered-black-teenager-emmett-till. See also Kenan Malik, "In Defense of Cultural Appropriation," *New York Times*, June 14, 2017; Lionel Shriver, "Lionel Shriver's Full Speech: 'I Hope the Concept of Cultural Appropriation Is a Passing Fad,'" *Guardian*, September 13, 2016.

16. Matthew Taylor, "'White Europe': 60,000 Nationalists March on Poland's Independence Day," *Guardian*, November 12, 2017; Anne Applebaum, "Why Neo-Fascists Are Making a Shocking Surge in Poland," *Washington Post*, November 13, 2017.

12. We the People

1. See Michela Wrong, *It's Our Turn to Eat: The Story of a Kenyan Whistle-Blower* (New York: HarperPerennial, 2010). See also Fukuyama, *Political Order and Political Decay*, 330–32.

2. Rogers M. Smith, *Political Peoplehood: The Roles of Values, Interests, and Identities* (Chicago: University of Chicago Press, 2015).

3. For a poignant account of both the richness of pre–World War I Vienna and the tragedy of its collapse, see Stefan Zweig, *The World of Yesterday* (Lincoln: University of Nebraska Press, 2013).

4. In the wake of President Trump's embrace of Vladimir Putin, a surprising number of Republicans have developed a favorable view of Russia, with a certain fringe asserting that they would trust Putin more than their fellow Americans who were liberal. Paul Reynolds, a Republican National Committee member from Alabama, was quoted as saying, "If I've got a choice of putting my welfare into the hands of Putin or the *Washington Post*, Putin wins every time." James Hohmann, "The Daily 202: As Roy Moore Declines to Step Aside, a Tale of Two Republican Parties Emerges," *Washington Post*, November 10, 2017; Zack Beauchamp, "Roy Moore Admires Vladimir Putin's Morality," *Vox*, December 8, 2017.

5. The rapidly developing states of East Asia had problems with corruption, but at levels generally lower than in other parts of the world. The elite focus on national development made possible the "developmental state" in countries such as Japan, South Korea, Singapore, and China. While such states have been said to exist in African countries such as Rwanda or Ethiopia, or in Chile under the Pinochet dictatorship, these have tended to be the exception rather than the rule. See Stephan Haggard, *Developmental States* (New York: Cambridge University Press, 2018).

6. See Francis Fukuyama, *Trust: The Social Virtues and the Creation of Prosperity* (New York: Free Press, 1995).

7. Ibid.; Robert D. Putnam, *Bowling Alone: The Collapse and Revival of American Community* (New York: Simon and Schuster, 2000).

8. This argument is made in Craig J. Calhoun, "Social Solidarity as a Problem for Cosmopolitan Democracy," in *Identities, Affiliations, and Allegiances*, ed. Seyla Benhabib, Ian Shapiro, and Danilo Petranovic (Cambridge: Cambridge University Press, 2007).

9. A classic argument for national identity as one of the necessary conditions of modern liberal democracy was made by Dankwart A. Rustow, "Transitions to Democracy: Toward a Dynamic Model," *Comparative Politics* 2 (1970): 337–63.

10. Zoltan L. Hajnal and Marisa Abrajano, *White Backlash: Immigration, Race, and American Politics* (Princeton, NJ: Princeton University Press, 2016).

11. Pierre Manent, "Democracy Without Nations?," *Journal of Democracy*

8 (1997): 92–102. See also Fukuyama, *Political Order and Political Decay*, 185–97.

12. On the origin of the Universal Declaration, see Mary Ann Glendon, *A World Made New: Eleanor Roosevelt and the Universal Declaration of Human Rights* (New York: Random House, 2001).

13. Martha C. Nussbaum, *For Love of Country: Debating the Limits of Patriotism* (Boston: Beacon Press, 1996); Craig J. Calhoun, "Imagining Solidarity: Cosmopolitanism, Constitutional Patriotism, and the Public Sphere," *Public Culture* 13 (1) (2002): 147–71; Samuel Scheffler, *Boundaries and Allegiances: Problems of Justice and Responsibility in Liberal Thought* (Oxford: Oxford University Press, 2000).

14. See Stewart Patrick, *Sovereignty Wars: Reconciling America with the World* (Washington, DC: Brookings Institution Press, 2017); Stephen D. Krasner, *Sovereignty: Organized Hypocrisy* (Princeton, NJ: Princeton University Press, 1999).

13. Stories of Peoplehood

1. This is argued in Sunil Khilnani, *The Idea of India* (New York: Farrar, Straus and Giroux, 1998).

2. This story is told in Fukuyama, *Political Order and Political Decay*, 322–34.

3. This section is based on my Latsis lecture "European Identity Challenges."

4. The theory of this view was outlined by Jürgen Habermas; see inter alia Habermas, *The Postnational Constellation: Political Essays* (Cambridge, MA: MIT Press, 2001); "Citizenship and National Identity: Some Reflections on the Future of Europe," *Praxis International* 12 (1) (1993): 1–19. See also Ghia Nodia, "The End of the Postnational Illusion," *Journal of Democracy* 28 (2017): 5–19.

5. On national identity in the EU, see Kathleen R. McNamara, *The Politics of Everyday Europe: Constructing Authority in the European Union* (Oxford: Oxford University Press, 2015).

6. T. Alexander Aleinikoff and Douglas B. Klusmeyer, eds., *From Migrants to Citizens: Membership in a Changing World* (Washington, DC: Carnegie Endowment for International Peace, 2000), 1–21; Gerhard Casper, "The Concept of National Citizenship in the Contemporary World: Identity or Volition?" (Hamburg, Germany: Bucerius Law School, 2008).

7. Aleinikoff and Klusmeyer, *From Migrants to Citizens*, 32–118.

8. Rogers Brubaker, *Citizenship and Nationhood in France and Germany* (Cambridge, MA: Harvard University Press, 1992).

9. Marc Morje Howard, *The Politics of Citizenship in Europe* (New York: Cambridge University Press, 2009), 119–34; Nergis Canefe, "Citizens v. Permanent Guests: Cultural Memory and Citizenship Laws in a Reunified Germany," *Citizenship Studies* 2 (3) (1998): 519–44.

10. Chikako Kashiwazaki, "Citizenship in Japan: Legal Practice and Contemporary Development," in Aleinikoff and Klusmeyer, *From Migrants to Citizens.*

11. Sara W. Goodman, "Fortifying Citizenship: Policy Strategies for Civic Integration in Western Europe," *World Politics* 64 (4) (2012): 659–98; Robert Leiken, *Europe's Angry Muslims: The Revolt of the Second Generation*, repr. ed. (Oxford: Oxford University Press, 2015). A number of his conclusions seem a bit dated today in light of recent terrorist attacks in France.

12. "Discussion Guide for the Naturalization Authorities—Status 01.09.2005," Country Commissioner for Data Protection Baden-Württemberg. September 1, 2005, https://www.baden-wuerttemberg.datenschutz.de /gesprachsleitfaden-fur-die-einburgerungsbehorden-stand-01-09-2005/. See also Simon McMahon, *Developments in the Theory and Practice of Citizenship* (Newcastle upon Tyne, U.K.: Cambridge Scholars, 2012), 29ff.

13. For empirical evidence of prejudice faced by French Muslims, see David Laitin, Claire L. Adida, and Marie-Anne Valfort, *Why Muslim Integration Fails in Christian-Heritage Societies* (Cambridge, MA: Harvard University Press, 2016).

14. For a history of UKIP see Robert Ford and Matthew Goodwin, *Revolt on the Right: Explaining Support for the Radical Right in Britain* (London: Routledge, 2014).

15. Alan G. R. Smith, *The Emergence of a Nation-State: The Commonwealth of England, 1529–1660* (London: Longman, 1984), 89.

16. Tweeted on August 12, 2017.

17. Quoted in Smith, *Political Peoplehood*, 150, 152.

18. Ibid. Paine quoted in Gerhard Casper, "Forswearing Allegiance," in *Jahrbuch des öffentlichen Rechts der Gegenwart*, ed. Peter Häberle (Tübingen, Germany: Mohr Siebeck, 2013), 703.

19. See Ramon Lopez, "Answering the Alt-Right," *National Affairs* 33 (2017): www.nationalaffairs.com/publications/detail/answering-the-alt-right.

20. William A. Galston, *Anti-Pluralism: The Populist Threat to Liberal Democracy* (New Haven, CT: Yale University Press, 2018), 39.

21. Samuel P. Huntington, *Who Are We? The Challenges to America's National Identity* (New York: Simon and Schuster, 2004), 59.

22. See for example Carlos Lozada, "Samuel Huntington, a Prophet for the Trump Era," *Washington Post*, July 18, 2017.

23. According to the OECD, Americans work an average of 34.29 hours per week, compared to an EU average of 33.23, and 39.79 in Korea. However, these averages include part-time workers, of whom there are proportionately more in the United States; average weekly hours for full-time U.S. workers is 47. See OECD (2018), Hours worked (indicator). DOI: 10.1787/47be1c78-en (accessed on February 14, 2018).

14. What Is to Be Done?

1. The U.S. citizenship oath is at https://www.uscis.gov/us-citizenship /naturalization-test/naturalization-oath-allegiance-united-states -america. For a detailed history of the naturalization oath, see Casper, "Forswearing Allegiance," in Häberle, *Jahrbuch*. See also T. Alexander Aleinikoff, "Between Principles and Politics: US Citizenship Policy," in Aleinikoff and Klusmeyer, *From Migrants to Citizens*.

2. Contrary to the oath of naturalization, the United States has come to permit dual citizenship as well. This was not the result of a deliberate act of Congress, but the result of various judicial and administrative decisions driven ultimately by political expediency. See Casper, "Concept of National Citizenship."

3. Bassam Tibi, "Why Can't They Be Democratic?," *Journal of Democracy* 19 (3) (2008): 43–48.

4. Something similar has happened in other multicultural societies in ways that sometimes get embodied in language. After the Acts of Union in 1707, when Scotland was incorporated into the United Kingdom, people in England began referring to themselves as British instead of English, an identity that included people in Wales, Scotland, and (at the time) Ireland. In the Russian language, the adjective *russkiy* means ethnic Russian, and the adjective *rossiyskiy* means a citizen of the Russian Federation, who could be a Muslim Chechen or a Dagestani.

5. "Muslim Identities and the School System in France and Britain: The Impact of the Political and Institutional Configurations on Islam-Related Education Policies," paper presented for the ECPR General Conference, Pisa, September 2007; Jenny Berglund, *Publicly Funded Islamic Education in Europe and the United States* (Washington, DC: Brookings Institution, 2015); Marie Parker-Johnson, "Equal Access to State Funding: The Case

of Muslim Schools in Britain," *Race, Ethnicity and Education* 5 (2010): 273–89.

6. Even in France there are exceptions; the French state supports religious schools in Alsace as one of the complex historical legacies of that contested region.

7. Despite some evidence that Proposition 227 had been followed by an increase in English acquisition by immigrant children, it was repealed by Proposition 58 in 2016. See Edward Sifuentes, "Proposition 227: 10 Years Later," *San Diego Union-Tribune*, November 8, 2008.

8. Daniel Jacobson, *Rights Across Borders: Immigration and the Decline of Citizenship* (Baltimore, MD: Johns Hopkins University Press, 1996), 8–11.

9. This situation changes the moment a foreigner reaches the territory of a given country. In the United States, Europe, and other liberal democracies, domestic law gives rights to noncitizens, including those who are undocumented. This creates strong incentives for migrants to reach the territory of a given country by any means possible, legal or illegal. It also gives states hoping to control their borders incentives to prevent them from doing so, by constructing physical barriers such as walls, interdiction on the high seas, or redirection to offshore jurisdictions where domestic law will not apply. See Casper, "Forswearing Allegiance," in Häberle, *Jahrbuch*; Moria Paz, "The Law of Walls," *European Journal of International Law* 28 (2) (2017): 601–24.

10. This was the proposed comprehensive immigration reform package suggested by the Brookings-Duke Immigration Policy Roundtable, "Breaking the Immigration Stalemate: From Deep Disagreements to Constructive Proposals," October 6, 2009.

11. *Vetocracy* refers to the way in which the American system of checks and balances permits well-organized minorities to veto decisions that get majority support. See Fukuyama, *Political Order and Political Decay*, chap. 34, pp. 488–505.

12. See Juan Pablo Cardenal et al., *Sharp Power: Rising Authoritarian Influence* (Washington, DC: National Endowment for Democracy, December 2017).

13. Neal Stephenson, *Snow Crash* (New York: Bantam Books, 1992).

BIBLIOGRAPHY

Abrajano, Marisa, and Zoltan L. Hajnal. *White Backlash: Immigration, Race, and American Politics*. Princeton, NJ: Princeton University Press, 2016.

Aleinikoff, T. Alexander, and Douglas B. Klusmeyer, eds. *From Migrants to Citizens: Membership in a Changing World*. Washington, DC: Carnegie Endowment for International Peace, 2000.

Barrett, Richard. *Foreign Fighters in Syria*. New York: Soufan Group, 2014.

Beauvoir, Simone de. *The Second Sex*. New York: Alfred A. Knopf, 1953.

Benhabib, Seyla, Ian Shapiro, and Danilo Petranovic, eds. *Identities, Affiliations, and Allegiances*. Cambridge: Cambridge University Press, 2007.

Berglund, Jenny. *Publicly Funded Islamic Education in Europe and the United States*. Washington, DC: Brookings Institution, 2015.

Berman, Sheri. "The Lost Left." *Journal of Democracy* 27 (4) (2016): 69–76.

Bock-Côté, Mathieu. *Le multiculturalisme comme religion politique*. Paris: Les Éditions du Cerf, 2016.

Brubaker, Rogers. *Citizenship and Nationhood in France and Germany*. Cambridge, MA: Harvard University Press, 1992.

Canefe, Nergis. "Citizens v. Permanent Guests: Cultural Memory and Citizenship Laws in a Reunified Germany." *Citizenship Studies* 2 (3) (1998): 519–44.

Casper, Gerhard. "The Concept of National Citizenship in the Contemporary World: Identity or Volition?" Hamburg, Germany: Bucerius Law School, 2008.

———. "Forswearing Allegiance." In *Jahrbuch des öffentlichen Rechts der Gegenwart*, edited by Peter Häberle. Tübingen, Germany: Mohr Siebeck, 2013.

Coates, Ta-Nehisi. *Between the World and Me*. New York: Spiegel and Grau, 2015.

Cramer, Katherine J. *The Politics of Resentment: Rural Consciousness and the Rise of Scott Walker*. Chicago: University of Chicago Press, 2016.

Crenshaw, Kimberlé Williams. "Mapping the Margins: Intersectionality, Identity Politics, and Violence Against Women of Color." *Stanford Law Review* 43:1241–99 (July 1991).

DeWaay, Bob. *Redefining Christianity: Understanding the Purpose Driven Movement*. Springfield, MO: 21st Century Press, 2006.

Ford, Robert, and Matthew Goodwin. *Revolt on the Right: Explaining Support for the Radical Right in Britain*. London: Routledge, 2014.

Fukuyama, Francis. "The End of History?" *National Interest* 16 (1989): 3–18.

———. *The End of History and the Last Man*. New York: Free Press, 1992.

———. *The Origins of Political Order: From Prehuman Times to the French Revolution*. New York: Farrar, Straus and Giroux, 2011.

———. "The Populist Surge." *American Interest* 13 (2018): 16–18.

———. *Our Posthuman Future: Consequences of the Biotechnology Revolution*. New York: Farrar, Straus and Giroux, 2001.

———. *Political Order and Political Decay: From the Industrial Revolution to the Globalization of Democracy*. New York: Farrar, Straus and Giroux, 2014.

———. *Trust: The Social Virtues and the Creation of Prosperity*. New York: Free Press, 1995.

Fuller, Robert W. *Dignity for All: How to Create a World Without Rankism*. Oakland, CA: Berrett-Koehler Publishers, 2008.

———. *Somebodies and Nobodies: Overcoming the Abuse of Rank*. Gabriola Island, British Columbia: New Society Publishers, 2003.

Furedi, Frank. "The Therapeutic University." *American Interest* 13 (1) (2017): 55–62.

———. *Therapy Culture: Cultivating Vulnerability in an Uncertain Age*. London: Routledge, 2004.

Galston, William A. *Anti-Pluralism: The Populist Threat to Liberal Democracy*. New Haven, CT: Yale University Press, 2018.

Gellner, Ernest. *Nations and Nationalism*. Ithaca, NY: Cornell University Press, 1983.

Glensy, Rex. "The Right to Dignity." *Columbia Human Rights Law Review* 43 (65) (2011): 65–142.

Goodman, Sara W. "Fortifying Citizenship: Policy Strategies for Civic Integration in Western Europe." *World Politics* 64 (4) (2012): 659–98.

Habermas, Jürgen. "Citizenship and National Identity: Some Reflections on the Future of Europe." *Praxis International* 12 (1) (1993): 1–19.

——. *The Postnational Constellation: Political Essays.* Cambridge, MA: MIT Press, 2001.

Haggard, Stephan. *Developmental States.* New York: Cambridge University Press, 2018.

Herder, Johann Gottfried von. *J. G. Herder on Social and Political Culture.* Cambridge: Cambridge University Press, 1969.

——. *Reflections on the Philosophy of the History of Mankind.* Chicago: University of Chicago Press, 1968.

Hochschild, Arlie Russell. *Strangers in Their Own Land: Anger and Mourning on the American Right.* New York: New Press, 2016.

Horowitz, Donald. *Ethnic Groups in Conflict.* Berkeley: University of California Press, 1985.

Howard, Marc Morje. *The Politics of Citizenship in Europe.* New York: Cambridge University Press, 2009.

Huntington, Samuel P. *Who Are We? The Challenges to America's National Identity.* New York: Simon and Schuster, 2004.

Jacobson, David. *Rights Across Borders: Immigration and the Decline of Citizenship.* Baltimore and London: Johns Hopkins University Press, 1996.

Kepel, Gilles. *Terror in France: The Rise of Jihad in the West.* Princeton, NJ: Princeton University Press, 2017.

Laitin, David, Claire L. Adida, and Marie-Anne Valfort. *Why Muslim Integration Fails in Christian-Heritage Societies.* Cambridge, MA: Harvard University Press, 2016.

Leiken, Robert. *Europe's Angry Muslims: The Revolt of the Second Generation.* Repr. ed. Oxford: Oxford University Press, 2015.

Lilla, Mark. *The Once and Future Liberal: After Identity Politics.* New York: HarperCollins, 2017.

Lindenberger, Herbert. *The History in Literature: On Value, Genre, Institutions.* New York: Columbia University Press, 1990.

Lochocki, Theo. "Germany's Left Is Committing Suicide by Identity Politics." *Foreign Policy,* January 23, 2018.

Lopez, Ramon. "Answering the Alt-Right." *National Affairs* 33 (2017).

Luther, Martin. *Christian Liberty.* Rev. ed. Edited by Harold J. Grimm. Philadelphia: Fortress Press, 1957.

Mann, Thomas E., and Norman J. Ornstein. *It's Even Worse Than It Looks:*

How the American Constitutional System Collided with the New Politics of Extremism. New York: Basic Books, 2012.

McMahon, Simon. *Developments in the Theory and Practice of Citizenship.* Newcastle upon Tyne, U.K.: Cambridge Scholars, 2012.

McNamara, Kathleen R. *The Politics of Everyday Europe: Constructing Authority in the European Union.* Oxford: Oxford University Press, 2015.

Milanovic, Branko. *Global Inequality: A New Approach for the Age of Globalization.* Cambridge, MA: Belknap Press, 2016.

Moyn, Samuel. "The Secret History of Constitutional Dignity." *Yale Human Rights and Development Journal* 17 (2) (2014): 39–73.

Murray, Charles. *Coming Apart: The State of White America, 1960–2010.* New York: Crown Forum, 2010.

Nodia, Ghia. "The End of the Postnational Illusion." *Journal of Democracy* 28 (2017): 5–19.

Nussbaum, Martha C. *For Love of Country: Debating the Limits of Patriotism.* Boston: Beacon Press, 1996.

Parker-Johnson, Marie. "Equal Access to State Funding: The Case of Muslim Schools in Britain." *Race, Ethnicity, and Education* 5 (2002): 273–89.

Paz, Moria. "The Law of Walls." *European Journal of International Law* 28 (2) (2017): 601–24.

Piketty, Thomas. *Capital in the Twenty-First Century.* Cambridge, MA: Belknap Press, 2014.

Polakow-Suransky, Sasha. *Go Back to Where You Came From: The Backlash Against Immigration and the Fate of Western Democracy.* New York: Nation Books, 2017.

Polsky, Andrew J. *The Rise of the Therapeutic State.* Princeton, NJ: Princeton University Press, 1991.

Putnam, Robert D. *Bowling Alone: The Collapse and Revival of American Community.* New York: Simon and Schuster, 2000.

———. *Our Kids: The American Dream in Crisis.* New York: Simon and Schuster, 2015.

Rieff, Philip. *The Triumph of the Therapeutic: Uses of Faith After Freud.* Chicago: University of Chicago Press, 1966.

Roy, Olivier. "EuroIslam: The Jihad Within?" *National Interest* 71 (2003): 63–74.

———. "France's Oedipal Islamist Complex." *Foreign Policy*, January 7, 2016.

———. "Who Are the New Jihadis?" *Guardian*, April 13, 2017.

Rustow, Dankwart A. "Transitions to Democracy: Toward a Dynamic Model." *Comparative Politics* 2 (1970): 337–63.

Scheffler, Samuel. *Boundaries and Allegiances: Problems of Justice and Responsibility in Liberal Thought.* Oxford: Oxford University Press, 2000.

Schuller, Robert H. *Self-Esteem: The New Reformation.* Waco, TX: Waco Books, 1982.

———. *Success Is Never Ending, Failure Is Never Final: How to Achieve Lasting Success Even in the Most Difficult Times.* New York: Bantam Books, 1990.

Smith, Alan G. R. *The Emergence of a Nation-State: The Commonwealth of England, 1529–1660.* London: Longman, 1984.

Smith, Rogers M. *Political Peoplehood: The Roles of Values, Interests, and Identities.* Chicago: University of Chicago Press, 2015.

Smith, Rogers M., and Sigal R. Ben-Porath, eds. *Varieties of Sovereignty and Citizenship.* Philadelphia: University of Pennsylvania Press, 2012.

Stern, Fritz. *The Politics of Cultural Despair: A Study in the Rise of German Ideology.* Berkeley: University of California Press, 1974.

Taylor, Charles. *The Ethics of Authenticity.* Cambridge, MA: Harvard University Press, 1992.

———. *Multiculturalism: Examining the Politics of Recognition."* Princeton, NJ: Princeton University Press, 1994.

———. *Sources of the Self: The Making of the Modern Identity.* Cambridge, MA: Harvard University Press, 1989.

Tibi, Bassam. "Why Can't They Be Democratic?" *Journal of Democracy* 19 (3) (2008): 43–48.

Trilling, Lionel. *Sincerity and Authenticity.* Cambridge, MA: Harvard University Press, 1972.

Warren, Rick. *The Purpose Driven Life: What on Earth Am I Here For?* Grand Rapids, MI: Zondervan, 2012.

Wright, Katie. *The Rise of the Therapeutic Society: Psychological Knowledge and the Contradictions of Cultural Change.* Washington, DC: New Academia Publishing, 2010.

Wrong, Michela. *It's Our Turn to Eat: The Story of a Kenyan Whistle-Blower.* New York: HarperPerennial, 2010.

Zaretsky, Robert. "Radicalized Islam, or Islamicized Radicalism?" *Chronicle of Higher Education* 62 (37) (2016).

Zweig, Stefan. *The World of Yesterday.* Lincoln: University of Nebraska Press, 2013.

INDEX

Page numbers in *italics* refer to tables.